PowerPoint

The Visual Learning Guide

Watch for these forthcoming titles from the same authors:

WINFAX PRO for Windows: The Visual Learning Guide
Ami Pro for Windows: The Visual Learning Guide

Available Now!

Windows 3.1: The Visual Learning Guide
WordPerfect 6 for DOS: The Visual Learning Guide
1-2-3 for Windows: The Visual Learning Guide
WordPerfect 6 for Windows: The Visual Learning Guide
Word for Windows 2: The Visual Learning Guide
Word for Windows 6: The Visual Learning Guide
Quicken 4 for Windows: The Visual Learning Guide
Excel 4 for Windows: The Visual Learning Guide
Excel 5 for Windows: The Visual Learning Guide

How to Order:

Quantity discounts are available from the publisher, Prima Publishing, P.O. Box 1260BK, Rocklin, CA 95677; Phone (916) 786-0426. On your letterhead include information concerning the intended use of the books and the number of books you wish to purchase.

PowerPoint
The Visual Learning Guide

Grace Joely Beatty, Ph.D.

David C. Gardner, Ph.D.

Prima Publishing
P.O. Box 1260BK
Rocklin, CA 95677

Library of Congress Catalog Card Number: 94-65674
ISBN: 1-55958-550-1

Executive Editor: Roger Stewart
Managing Editor: Neweleen A. Trebnik
Project Manager: Becky Freeman
Production and Layout: Marian Hartsough Associates
Interior Design: Grace Joely Beatty, S. Linda Beatty, David C. Gardner,
    Laurie Stewart, and Kim Bartusch
Technical Editing: Linda Miles
Cover Design: Page Design, Inc.
Color Separations: Ocean Quigley
Index: Katherine Stimson

Prima Publishing
Rocklin, CA 95677-1260

94 95 96 97 RRD 10 9 8 7 6 5 4 3 2 1

Printed in the United States of America

Acknowledgments

We are deeply indebted to reviewers around the country who gave generously of their time to test every step in the manuscript. Joseph Beatty, David Coburn, Ray Holder, Don Linehan, David Sauer, and David Sieverding cannot be thanked enough!

Carolyn Holder, Linda Beatty, and Anne-Barbara Norris are our in-house production team, reviewers, proofreaders, screen capturers, and friends. They, along with Ray Holder and Margaret Short, keep us functioning.

We are especially indebted to Linda Beatty. Her experience in desktop publishing and all things "artistic" was invaluable in developing the models used in this book.

We are personally and professionally delighted to work with everyone at Prima Publishing, especially Roger Stewart, executive editor; Neweleen Trebnik, managing editor; Becky Freeman, project manager; Debbie Parisi, publicity coordinator; and Kim Bartusch, production coordinator.

Linda Miles, technical editor; Becky Whitney, copy editor; Ocean Quigley, color separator; Marian Hartsough, Edwin Smith, and Barbara Lewis, interior layout; and Paul Page, cover design, contributed immensely to the final product.

Bill Gladstone and Matt Wagner, of Waterside Productions, created the idea for this series. Their faith in us has never wavered.

Joseph and Shirley Beatty made this series possible. We can never repay them.

Asher Schapiro has always been there when we needed him.

Paula Gardner Capaldo and David Capaldo have been terrific. Thanks, Joshua and Jessica, for being such wonderful kids! Our project humorist, Mike Bumgardner, always came through when we needed a boost!

We could not have met the deadlines without the technical support of Ray Holder, our electrical genius, Diana M. Balelo, Frank E. Straw, Daniel W. Terhark, and Martin J. O'Keefe, of Computer Service & Maintenance, our computer wizards, and John Langhans, of PowerPoint technical support staff. Thank you all!

CONTENTS

Customize Your Learning

Prima Visual Learning Guides are not like any other computer books you have ever seen. They are based on our years in the classroom, our corporate consulting, and our research at Boston University on the best ways to teach technical information to nontechnical learners. Most important, this series is based on the feedback of a panel of reviewers from across the country who range in computer knowledge from "panicked at the thought" to sophisticated.

This is not an everything-you've-ever-wanted-to-know-about PowerPoint 4 for Windows book. It is designed to give you the information you need to perform basic (and some not so basic) functions with confidence and skill. It is a book that our reviewers claim makes it "really easy" for anyone to learn PowerPoint 4 for Windows quickly.

Each chapter is illustrated with full-color screens to guide you through every task. The combination of screens, step-by-step instructions, and pointers make it impossible for you to get lost or confused as you follow along on your own computer. You can either work through from beginning to end or skip around to master the skills you need. If you have a specific goal you want to accomplish now, choose it from the following section.

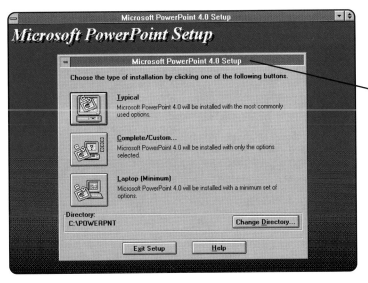

SELECT YOUR GOALS

❖ I would like help installing PowerPoint 4.0

Go to the Appendix, "Installing PowerPoint 4.0.

❖ I'm new to PowerPoint, and I want to learn how to create a basic presentation.

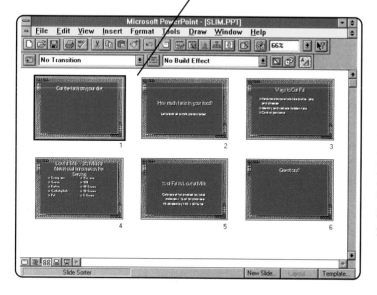

Turn to Part I, "Creating a Basic Presentation," to learn how to take advantage of PowerPoint's predesigned slide layouts and templates, how to edit text and work with text blocks, how to print paper copies of your presentation, and how to send your presentation to a service bureau to be made into slides.

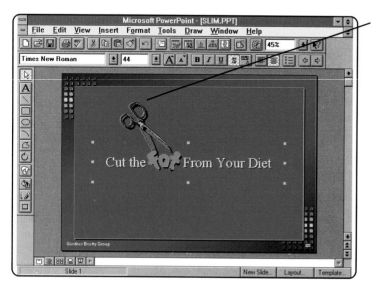

❖ I want to know how to customize a presentation.

Turn to Part II, "Creating a Customized Presentation," to learn how to work with clip art, how to use the drawing program in PowerPoint, and how to create special effects with WordArt.

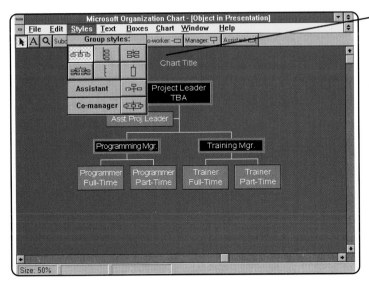

❖ I want to know how to create graphs, tables, and organization charts in PowerPoint.

Part III, "Graphs, Tables, and Charts," will show you how to create these elements in PowerPoint. You will also learn how to import a worksheet or graph from Excel.

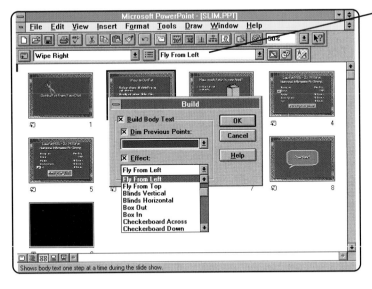

❖ I want to know how to run a slide show from my computer.

Part IV, "Running a Slide Show," deals with setting up and rehearsing a slide show, creating special transition effects for a computer-generated show, and learning the special information you need in order to take your show on the road.

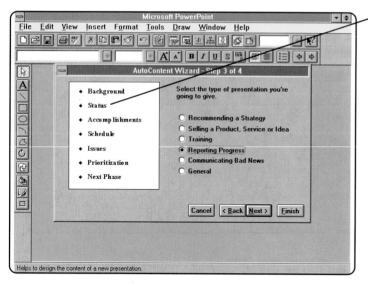

❖ I want to know how to use some of the special features of PowerPoint 4, like the AutoContent Wizard.

Part IV, "Special Features," deals with using the AutoContent Wizard. It also shows you how to customize the master slide.

Program Manager

Part I: Creating a Basic Presentation

Beginning a Basic Presentation

Gone are the endless hours of laying out and formatting presentation materials. PowerPoint 4.0 has 21 preformatted layout designs that automatically center text, create bulleted lists, and import clip art and charts. You can even use a Spelling Checker to help proofread. In this chapter you will do the following:

❖ Create a new presentation

❖ Choose predesigned layouts from AutoLayout

❖ Enter text

❖ Use the Spelling Checker

OPENING PowerPoint FOR THE FIRST TIME

1. **Type win** at the C:\> (C prompt) on your screen to boot up Windows, if it is not already on your screen. Windows provides for tremendous customization, so you will probably have different group icons at the bottom of your screen than the ones you see in this example.

2. **Click twice** on the **icon** for the group that contains PowerPoint 4.0. In this example, it is the **Microsoft Office** group icon.

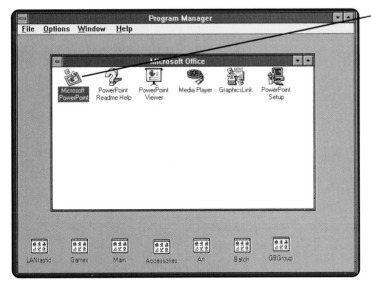

3. Click twice on the **PowerPoint icon**. After a lengthy hourglass intermission, a Microsoft PowerPoint message box will appear.

The first time you open PowerPoint, you will be asked if you want to take the Quick Preview tour.

Taking the Quick Preview Tour

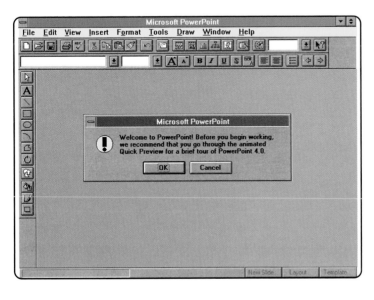

1a. Click on **Cancel** if you don't want to take the tour. You will go directly to the screen you see at the bottom of the next page. If you don't do the Quick Preview now, you can still see it at any time by choosing the Quick Preview command from the Help menu.

1b. Or, if you would like to take the animated tour of PowerPoint 4.0, **click** on **OK**. A Quick Preview opening screen will appear.

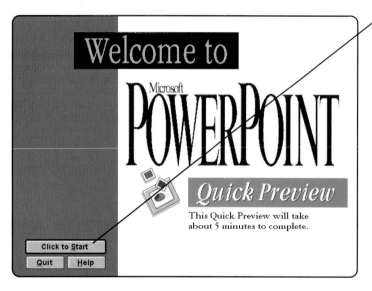

2. Click on **Click to Start**.

If you want to discontinue the tour at any time, click on Quit. A new presentation screen with a Tip of the Day dialog box will appear, as you see in the next example.

Viewing the Tip of the Day

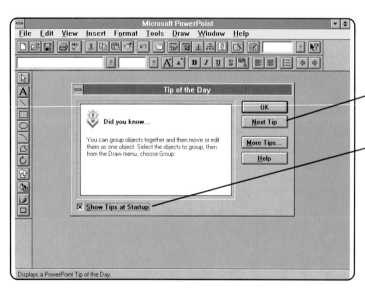

Every time you boot up PowerPoint, you will see a Tip of the Day.

1. Click on **Next Tip** to see another tip.

If it drives you crazy to see a Tip of the day every time you start PowerPoint, **click** on **Show Tips at Startup** to *remove* the X from the box. This will prevent Power-Point from automatically showing tips.

If you choose this option, you can still see tips by choosing the Tip of the Day command from the Help menu.

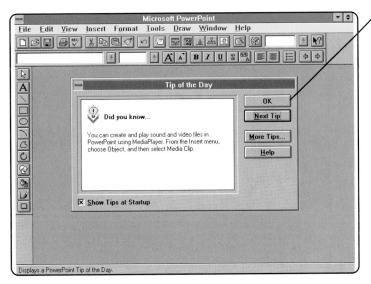

2. **Click** on **OK** to close the dialog box. A PowerPoint dialog box will appear on your screen.

CREATING A NEW PRESENTATION

You can use any one of the options in the New Presentation dialog box to begin a new presentation. In this section, you will choose Blank Presentation. "Blank" refers to the fact that the presentation is not yet dressed up with a predesigned color scheme. You will dress up your presentation in Chapter 3, "Choosing a Predesigned Template." You will learn how to use all the options on this menu as you go through the chapters in this book.

1. **Click** on **Blank Presentation** to insert a dot in the circle.

2. **Click** on **OK**. The New Slide dialog box will appear.

USING AutoLayout

AutoLayout contains 21 preformatted layout designs that are set up to center text, make a bulleted list, and add clip art and charts. You can mix AutoLayout slides with individually designed slides. In this chapter, you will create five slides. "Slides," by the way, is a generic term. You will decide whether your presentation will be slides, overheads, or an on-screen presentation in Chapter 3.

Creating a Title Slide

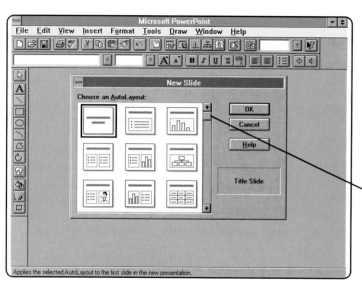

1. **Move** the mouse arrow to the **scroll button**.

2. **Press and hold** the mouse button as you **drag** it to the bottom of the scroll bar.

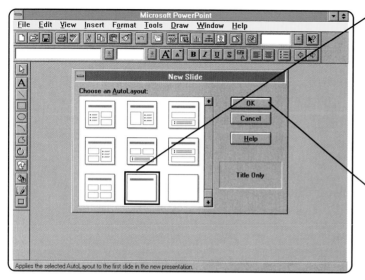

3. **Click** on the **Title Only slide**. A dark border will appear around the slide to show that it is selected.

Notice that a description of the slide appears to the right.

4. **Click** on **OK**. After a pause, the Presentation screen will appear.

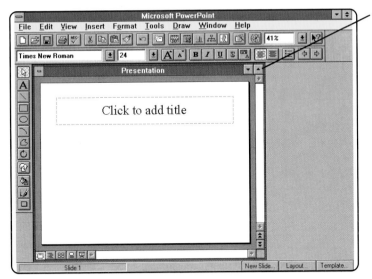

5. **Click** on the **Maximize button** (▲) to maximize the Presentation dialog box.

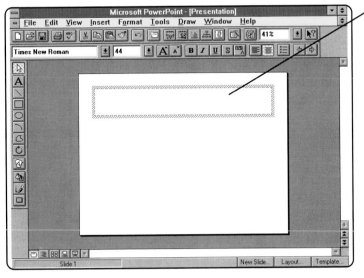

6. **Click anywhere inside** the dotted-line border. The instructions will disappear, the border will become candy-striped, and the cursor will flash in the center of the box. This box is called a *text block*.

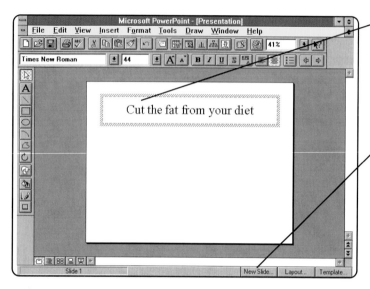

7. Type Cut the fat from your diet. (Don't include the period.)

Notice that the title automatically centers itself.

8. Click on **New Slide** so that you can create the next slide. The New Slide dialog box will appear.

Creating a Slide with a Title and Subtitle

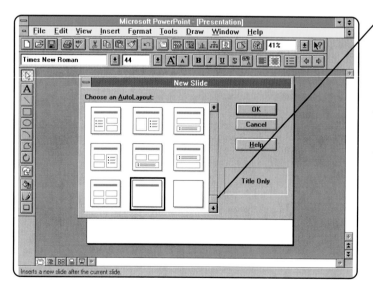

1. Move the mouse arrow to the **scroll button** on the scroll bar.

2. Press and hold the mouse button as you **drag** the scroll button to the **top** of the scroll bar.

3. **Click** on the **Title slide** in the upper left corner.

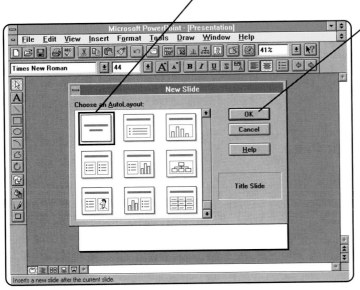

4. **Click** on **OK**. The Presentation screen will appear.

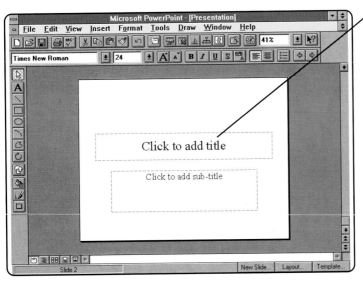

5. **Click anywhere inside** the **title text block**. The instructions will disappear, a candy-striped border will appear, and the cursor will flash in the center of the block.

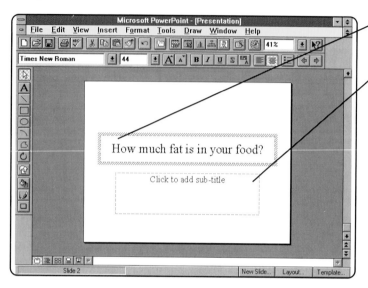

6. Type How much fat is in your food?

7. Click inside the **subtitle** text block. The cursor will flash in the center of the text block.

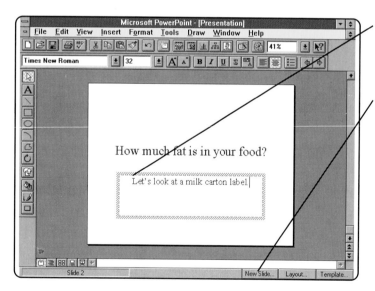

8. Type Let's look at a milk carton label. (Include the period.)

9. Click on the New Slide **button**. The New Slide dialog box will appear.

Creating a Bulleted List

1. Click on the **Bulleted List slide** if it is not already selected. (It is the middle slide in the top row.)

2. Click on **OK**. The Presentation screen will appear.

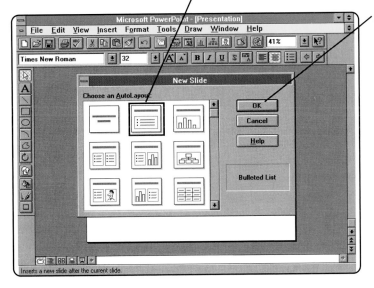

3. Click on the **title block**. The cursor will flash in the center of the text block.

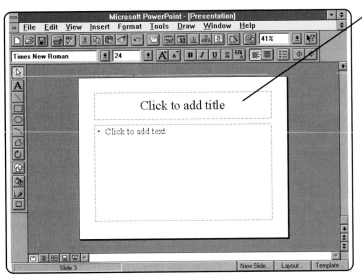

4. Type Ways to Cut Fat. (Don't include the period.)

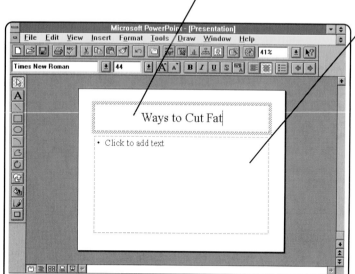

5. Click anywhere inside the **bulleted text block**.

Notice that after you click, the instructional text disappears but the bullet remains. The cursor will flash to the right of the bullet.

6. Type Reduce obvious fats like butter, oils, and cheese. (Don't include the period.)

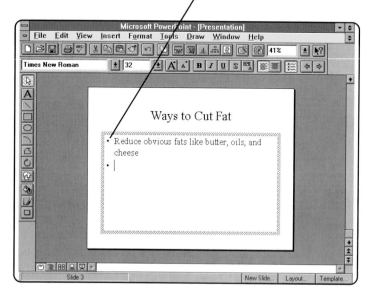

Notice that the word "cheese" automatically wraps to the second line and indents.

7. Press Enter. Another bullet will appear.

8. Type Identify and reduce hidden fats. (Don't include the period.)

9. Press Enter. Another bullet will appear.

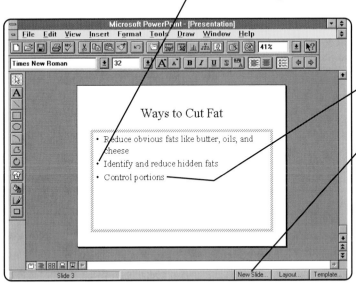

10. Type Control portions. (Don't include the period.)

11. Click on the **New Slide button**. The New Slide dialog box will appear.

Creating a Slide with Two Columns of Text

1. Click on the **2 Column Text slide**. (It is the first slide in the second row.)

2. Click on **OK**.

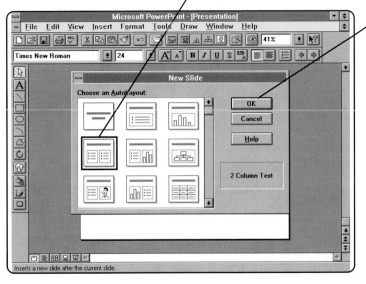

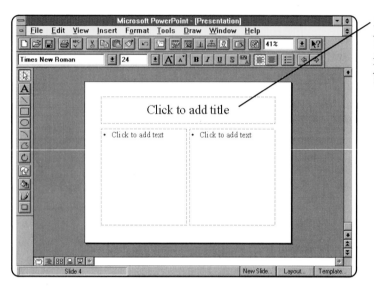

3. Click inside the **title block**. The cursor will flash in the center of the text block.

4. Type Lowfat Milk - 2% Milkfat and then **press Enter** to add a line to the text block.

5. Type Nutritional Information Per Serving. (Don't include the period.) Notice that the text automatically wraps to a new line. In Chapter 5, you will change the font in the title block so that it will not obscure the text below it.

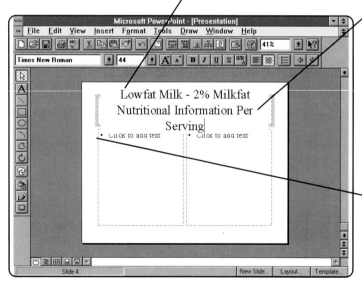

6. Click anywhere inside the **left text block**. The text will disappear, but the bullet will remain. The cursor will flash to the right of the bullet.

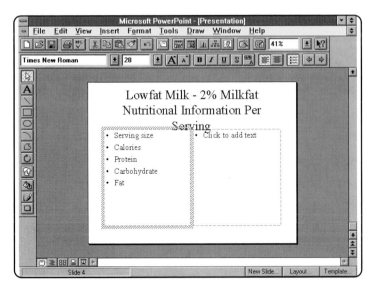

7. Type the following lines and **press** the **Enter key** between each item to create a new bullet:

> **Serving size**
> **Calories**
> **Protein**
> **Carbohydrate**
> **Fat**

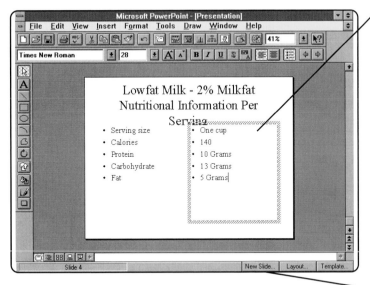

8. Click inside the **right text block.**

9. Type the following lines and **press** the **Enter key** between each item to create a new bullet:

> **One cup**
> **140**
> **10 Grams**
> **13 Grams**
> **5 Grams**

10. Click on the **New Slide button.** The New Slide dialog box will appear.

Creating a Slide with Two Text Areas

Don't feel limited by the label that AutoLayout gives to the predesigned slides. If the general layout of the slide is appropriate, use it. You can expand a text block to contain more lines of type than you see in the example.

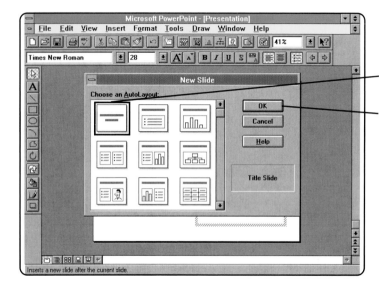

1. **Click** on the **Title slide**.

2. **Click** on **OK**.

3. **Click inside** the **title block**. The cursor will flash in the center of the text block.

4. **Type % of Fat in Lowfat Milk**. (Don't include the period.)

5. **Click inside** the **subtitle block.**

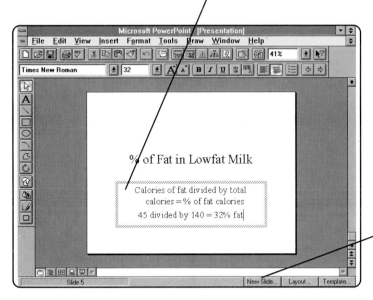

6. **Type Calories of fat divided by total calories = % of fat calories**. (Don't include the period.)

7. **Press Enter.**

8. **Type 45 divided by 140 = 32% fat**. (Don't include the period.)

9. **Click** on the **New Slide button.** The New Slide dialog box will appear.

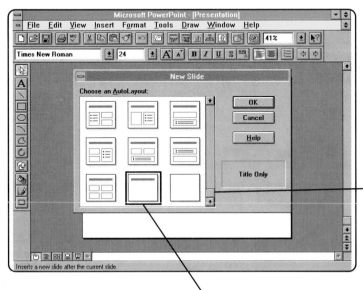

Creating a Slide with One Text Line

1. **Move** the mouse arrow to the **scroll button** on the scroll bar.

2. **Press and hold** the mouse button as you **drag** the scroll button to the **bottom** of the screen.

3. **Click twice** on the **Title Only slide**. The Presentation screen will appear. (Clicking twice is the same as clicking once plus clicking on OK.)

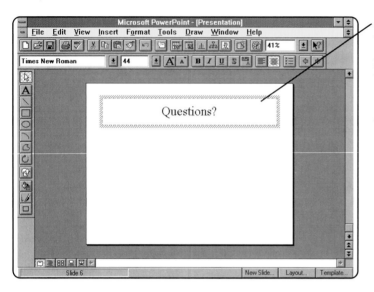

4. **Click inside** the **title block**. The cursor will flash in the center of the text block.

5. **Type Questions?**

USING THE SPELLING CHECKER

Be sure to check your spelling. Few occasions are more embarrassing than having your spelling errors seen larger than life by an entire audience. The Spelling Checker in PowerPoint works the same way it does in Word and other Windows-based word-processing programs.

Starting the Spelling Checker

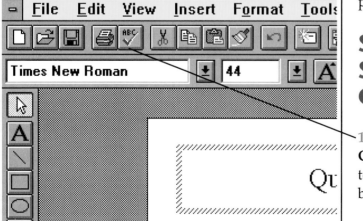

1. **Click** on the **Spelling Checker button** on the toolbar. The Spelling dialog box will appear.

Adding a Word to the Custom Dictionary

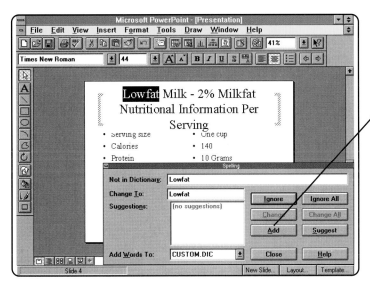

In the presentation you just typed, there are two words that can be added to the Custom dictionary.

1. Click on **Add** to add Lowfat to the Custom dictionary.

2. When the Spelling Checker identifies Milkfat as an unknown word, **click** on **Add** to add it to the Custom dictionary.

Because there are no other misspelled or unknown words, a PowerPoint message box will tell you that it has finished checking the spelling.

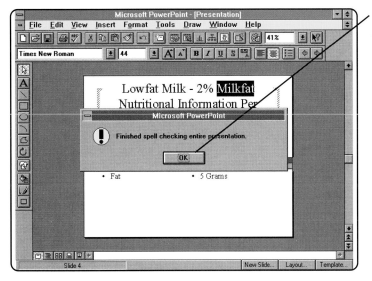

3. Click on **OK** to close the Spelling Checker.

You'll name and save the presentation in the next chapter.

Naming, Saving, Closing, and Opening a File

PowerPoint uses standard Windows-based commands to name, save, and close a file. In this chapter you will do the following:

❖ Name and save a file

❖ Close a file

❖ Close PowerPoint

❖ Open an existing presentation

NAMING AND SAVING A FILE

In this section, you will name the presentation you created in Chapter 2.

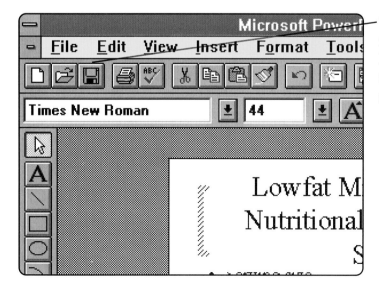

1. **Click** on the **Save button** in the toolbar. Because you have not named the file, the Save As dialog box will appear.

2. Type slim. It will replace the highlighted text. (Filenames can have up to eight characters with no spaces.)

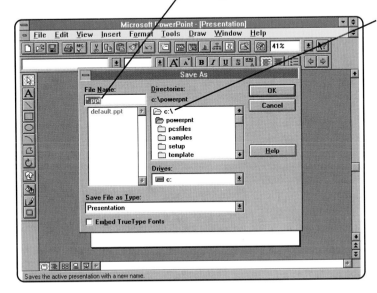

The open file folders next to "c:\" and "powerpnt" indicate that the file will be saved on the C drive in the powerpnt directory.

It doesn't matter if you type the filename in capital or small letters. The filename will appear in capital letters on the slide presentation screen. PowerPoint will automatically add the .ppt extension to identify it as belonging to the program.

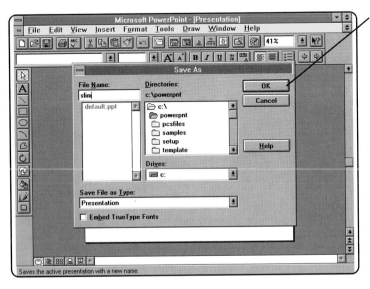

3. Click on **OK**. The Summary Info screen will appear.

Filling In the Summary Info

When you save for the first time, PowerPoint displays the Summary Info dialog box. Filling in this dialog box is optional. However, the information you add will be useful if you want to search for a file.

Notice that the title has already been filled in from the first "title" slide you created in Chapter 1.

1. Click in the **Subject** box and **type Fat Content**.

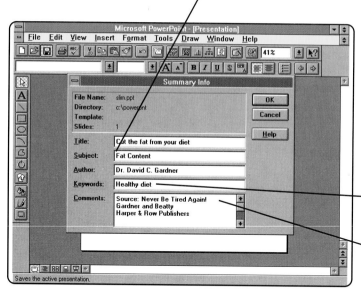

The author's name is the name that was typed during setup (in this example, Dr. David C. Gardner). You can change this by dragging the mouse pointer over the name and highlighting it. Then type the name you want.

2. Click in the **Keywords** box. **Type Healthy diet**.

3. Press Tab to move to the Comments box and type the following:

> **Source: Never Be Tired Again!**
> **Gardner and Beatty**
> **Harper & Row Publishers.**

4. Click on **OK**. The dialog box will disappear.

CLOSING A FILE

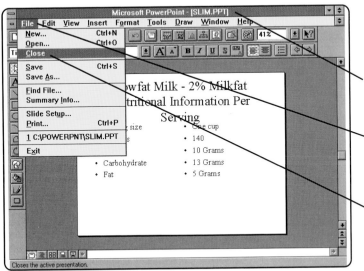

In this section, you will close the SLIM file you created in Chapter 1.

Notice the filename in the title bar.

1. **Click** on **File** in the menu bar. A pull-down menu will appear.

2. **Click** on **Close**. The SLIM file will close and you will see a blank PowerPoint screen.

CLOSING POWERPOINT FOR WINDOWS

1. **Click** on **File** in the menu bar. A pull-down menu will appear.

Notice that the file you just saved is listed on the File pull-down menu. This menu lists the four most recent files on which you have worked. You can open a file by clicking on its name on this menu.

2. **Click** on **Exit**. PowerPoint will close and you will be back at the Microsoft Office group window.

OPENING AN EXISTING PRESENTATION

1. Click twice on the **Microsoft PowerPoint 4.0 icon** to open the program. After a pause, the Tip of the Day dialog box will appear if you did not turn it off.

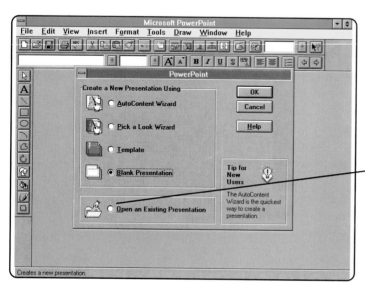

2. Click on **OK**. The PowerPoint dialog box will appear.

3. Click on **Open an Existing Presentation** to place a dot in the circle.

4. Click on **OK**. The Open dialog box will appear with a list of saved files.

5. Click on **slim.ppt** to highlight it. The filename will appear in the File Name text box, and the first slide will appear in the sample box.

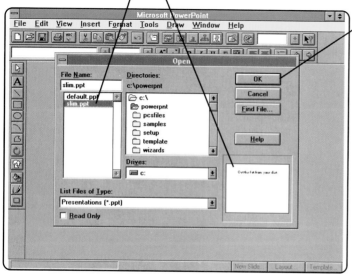

6. Click on **OK**. A Microsoft PowerPoint screen will appear, showing the first slide in your presentation.

In the next chapter, you will use Pick a Look Wizard to dress up your presentation.

Choosing a Predesigned Template

You can dress up your presentation by choosing from a collection of predesigned templates in Pick a Look Wizard. These templates include special graphics designs and color schemes. With Pick a Look Wizard, you can add supplementary materials such as speaker's notes, handouts, and an outline to your presentation materials. You can customize each of these with your company name (or other identifying text) as well as the date and page number. In this chapter you will do the following:

❖ Choose a template from Pick a Look Wizard

❖ Determine the optional text to be included on slides, notes, handouts, and outlines

❖ Learn how to remove a predesigned template

OPENING PICK A LOOK WIZARD

You can choose a template from Pick a Look Wizard before you enter the text for your presentation. Or you can enter text first, and then choose a template, as you will do in this chapter.

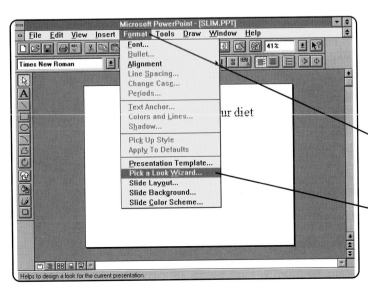

1. **Open slim.ppt** if it is not already open.

2. **Click** on **Format** in the menu bar. A pull-down menu will appear.

3. **Click** on **Pick a Look Wizard**. The Pick A Look Wizard - Step 1 of 9 dialog box will appear.

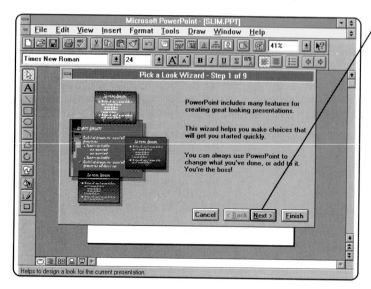

4. **Click** on the **Next>
button**. The Pick a Look
Wizard - Step 2 of 9 dialog
box will appear.

Notice that you can choose
from four types of
presentations:

❖ Black and White
Overheads

❖ Color Overheads

❖ On-Screen Presentation

❖ 35mm Slides

In this example, you will choose 35mm Slides.
However, you can change to a different type of
presentation at any point by opening this dialog box
and clicking on the appropriate choice. If you plan to
print a copy of the slides and use them to make
overhead transparencies,
we suggest that you select
Black and White Overheads
unless you have a color
printer and color
photocopier.

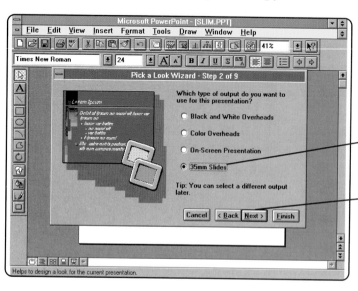

5. **Click** on **35mm Slides** to
insert a dot into the circle.

6. **Click** on the **Next>
button**. The Pick a Look
Wizard - Step 3 of 9 dialog
box will appear.

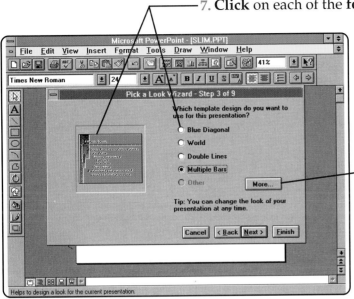

7. **Click** on each of the **four choices** listed in the dialog box and watch as the format is displayed in the sample to the left.

There are many more choices from which to choose.

8. **Click** on **More**. The Presentation Template dialog box will appear.

Selecting a Template

You can change the color and style of the master template to any one of PowerPoint's predesigned color templates.

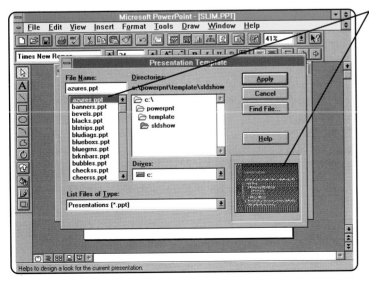

1. **Click** on **azures.ppt**. A sample of this particular template will appear in the sample box.

2. **Press** the ↓ **key** on your keyboard to scroll through the selection of templates.

In this chapter, we will use multboxs.ppt as the example. You can select another template, but your screens will differ from the ones you see here.

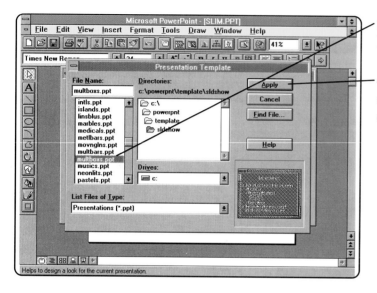

3. **Click** on **multboxs.ppt** to highlight it.

4. **Click** on **Apply**. The Pick a Look Wizard - step 3 of 9 dialog box will appear.

ADDING NOTES, HANDOUTS, AND OUTLINE PAGES TO YOUR PRESENTATION

With Pick a Look Wizard, you can print full-page versions of slides, speaker's notes, handout copies of the slides, and outline pages. PowerPoint can also add your company name (or other text), the date, and page number to slides and other supplementary materials. You can customize the text and delete any information you do not want to show.

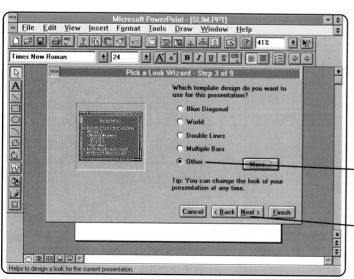

Notice that Other has been selected.

1. **Click** on **Next>**. The Step 4 of 9 dialog box will appear.

Notice that all four options have been selected and an example of each is shown, starting with a full-page slide in the upper left corner and continuing clockwise to an outline page. In these examples, you will keep all four options.

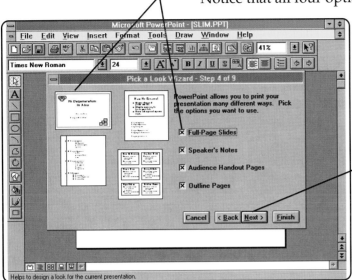

2. **Click** on **Next>**. The Pick a Look Wizard - Slide Options dialog box will appear.

Customizing Slides

Notice that if you typed a company name during installation, it appears here. You have the option of not including it or changing it to other text. This example will include the company name and page numbers.

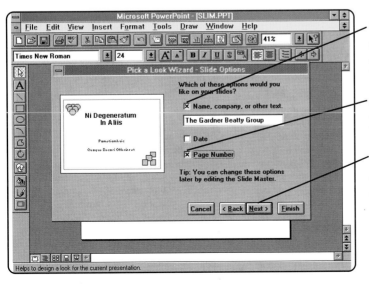

1. **Click** on **Name, company, or other text** to place an ✗ in the box.

2. **Click** on **Page Number** to place an ✗ in the box.

3. **Click** on **Next>**. The Pick a Look - Notes Option dialog box will appear.

Customizing Speaker's Notes

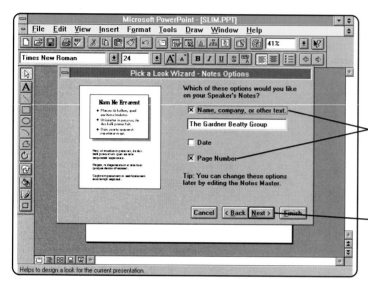

A speaker's note shows a copy of the slide at the top of the page with room for notes at the bottom. (More on this in Chapter 9.)

1. **Click** on **Name, company, or other text** and **Page Number** to place Xs in the boxes.

2. **Click** on **Next>**. The Pick a Look Wizard - Handout Options dialog box will appear.

Customizing Handouts

You can provide your audience with copies of your slides by using the Handouts option. (More on handouts in Chapter 9.)

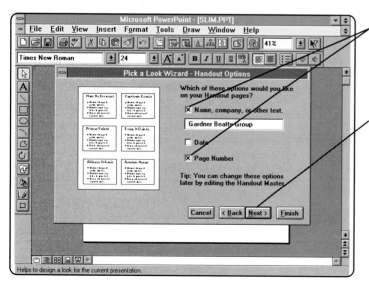

1. **Click** on **Name, company, or other text** and **Page Number** to place Xs in the boxes.

2. **Click** on **Next>**. The Pick a Look Wizard - Outlines Options dialog box will appear.

Customizing the Outline

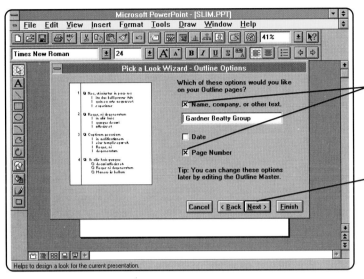

The Outline option prints the text of your slides in outline form.

1. **Click** on **Name, company, or other text** and **Page Number** to place Xs in the boxes.

2. **Click** on **Next>**. The Pick a Look Wizard - Step 9 of 9 dialog box will appear.

Applying the Pick a Look Template

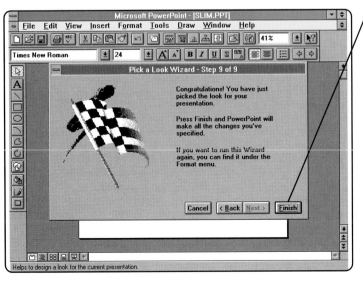

1. **Click** on **Finish** to see the new design you have selected for your presentation. It may take a few seconds to show on your screen.

You can choose another predesigned template at any time by clicking on Format in the menu bar and then clicking on Pick a Look Wizard. However, there is one minor drawback to doing this. If you open Pick a Look Wizard again for this presentation, it will not

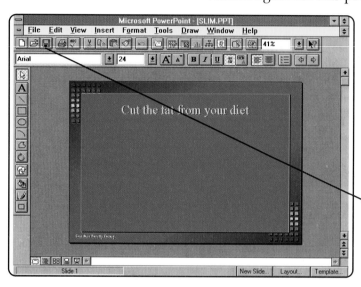

remember any of the options you selected for color scheme or supplementary materials. You must go through each screen and make your selections all over again.

SAVING THE FILE

1. Click on the **Save button** in the toolbar. The slim.ppt file is now ready for Chapter 5, "Editing and Styling Text."

REMOVING A PICK A LOOK WIZARD DESIGN

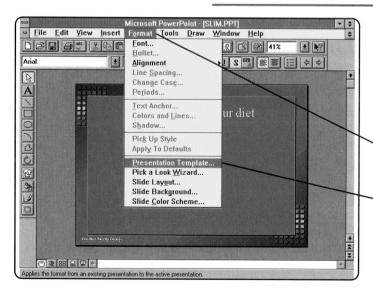

You can change a design by using Pick a Look Wizard, but you cannot remove one. To remove a Pick a Look design, follow these steps:

1. Click on **Format** in the menu bar.

2. Click on **Presentation Template**.

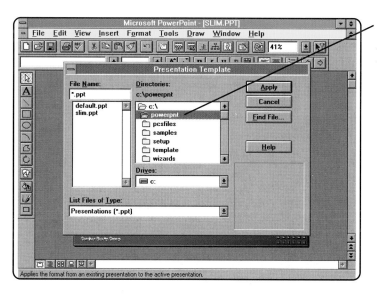

3. **Click twice** on **powerpnt**. A list of files will appear on the left.

4. **Click** on **default**.

If you do not want to remove the design at this point, click on Cancel. If you click on Apply, the Pick a Look design will be completely removed from your slides. You will have to repeat all of the steps in this chapter to apply a new design.

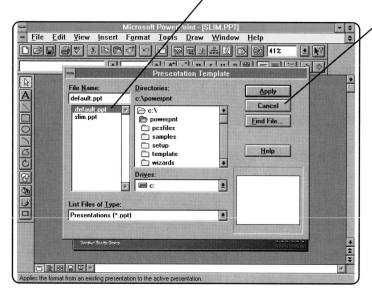

Viewing, Moving, Copying, and Adding Slides

You can move slides in PowerPoint almost as if you were using a slide sorter. Copying and deleting slides is as easy as clicking your mouse. You can zoom in to see a close-up of a slide or zoom out to see a number of slides at one time. In this chapter you will do the following:

❖ Change to different views

❖ Copy, move, and delete a slide

❖ Use the Zoom feature

CHANGING TO SLIDE SORTER VIEW

1. **Place** your **mouse arrow** over the Slide Sorter View button, which is the third button from the left at the bottom of your screen. Notice that a pop-up *tooltip* box tells you the name of the button. A description of the button's function appears in the status bar at the very bottom of your screen. (Try this with other buttons at the top and bottom of your screen.)

2. **Click** on the **Slide Sorter View button**. The slides in your presentation will be shown in a bird's-eye view on the screen.

Notice that slide 1 has a bold border to show that it is the slide that is currently selected.

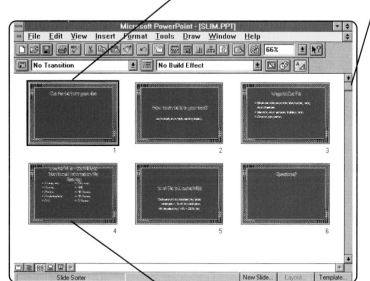

If you have more than six slides, you can view them by dragging the scroll button down the scroll bar.

COPYING A SLIDE WITH THE COPY BUTTON

There are several ways to copy a slide in PowerPoint. Here is one.

1. **Click** on **slide 4** to select it.

2. **Click** on the **Copy button**. (You can also click on Edit in the menu bar and then click on Copy on the pull-down menu.)

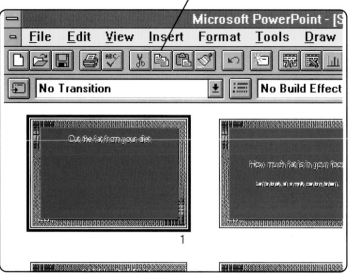

3. **Click** once **to the right of slide 4**. Notice the insertion line appears between slides 4 and 5. Unless you click somewhere else, the copied slide will be pasted here.

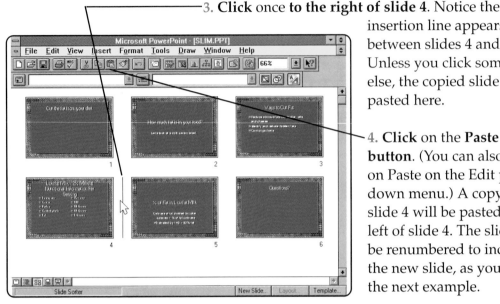

4. **Click** on the **Paste button**. (You can also click on Paste on the Edit pull-down menu.) A copy of slide 4 will be pasted to the left of slide 4. The slides will be renumbered to include the new slide, as you see in the next example.

USING UNDO

Let's say you decided not to insert this copy of slide 4 after all. PowerPoint makes it easy to undo as long as you use the Undo option before you perform any other function.

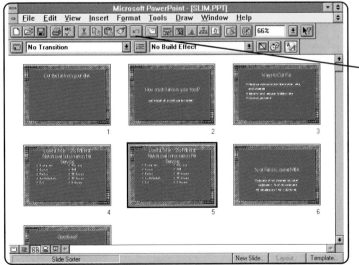

1. **Click** on the **Undo button**. The slide will be deleted, and the other slides renumbered back to the way they were.

MOVING A SLIDE

The drag-and-drop feature of PowerPoint lets you move slides as if you were using a slide sorter.

1. **Click** on **slide 2** to select it.

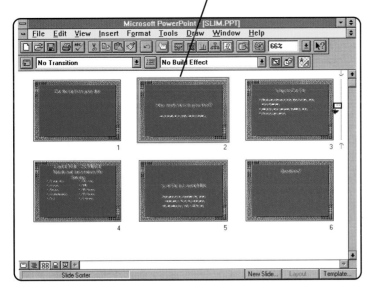

2. **Press and hold** your mouse button. Then drag the mouse pointer to the **right of slide 3**. You will see a tiny slide being dragged. A dotted vertical insertion line will appear to the right of slide 3.

3. **Release** the mouse button. Slide 2 will be in the slide 3 position, and the slides will be renumbered accordingly.

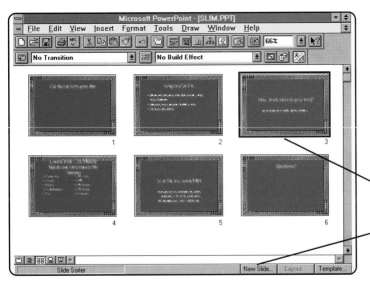

INSERTING A SLIDE

When you add a slide to a presentation it is inserted to the right of whatever slide is already selected.

1. **Click** on **slide 3** if it is not currently selected.

2. **Click** on the **New Slide button**. The New Slide dialog box will appear.

3. Drag the **scroll button** to the top of the scroll bar if it is not already there.

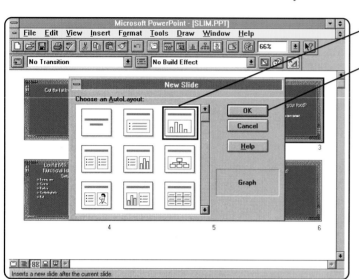

4. Click on the **Graph** slide.

5. Click on **OK**. The Slide Sorter view will appear with an empty slide as slide 4. The empty text blocks on this slide do not show in the Slide Sorter view. They show only in Slide view.

Your screen will look like the example below.

DELETING A SLIDE

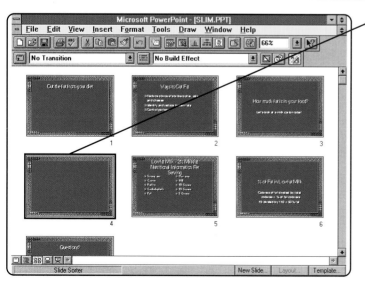

1. Click on **slide 4** if it is not already selected.

2. Press the **delete key** (or Backspace key) to delete it. The slide will disappear instantly!

USING THE ZOOM FEATURE

The standard Slide Sorter view shows six slides. If you have more than six slides in your presentation, you can use this feature to see more slides at the same time.

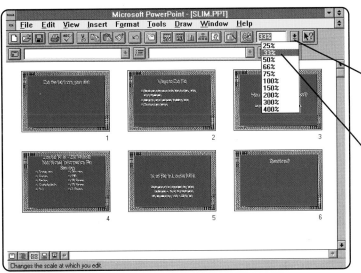

1. **Click** on the ↓ to the right of the Zoom Control box in the toolbar.

2. **Click** on **33%**. The slides will appear in a 33% view.

You can also use the menu bar to zoom.

3. **Click** on **View** in the menu bar. A pull-down menu will appear.

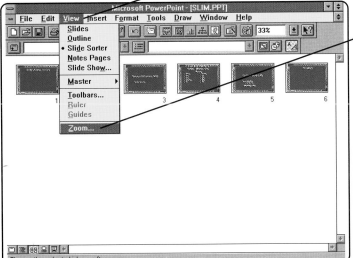

4. **Click** on **Zoom**. The Zoom dialog box will appear.

5. **Click** on **66%**.

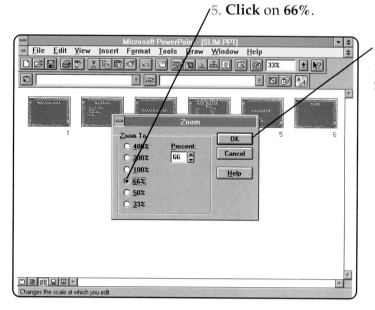

6. **Click** on **OK**. You will be returned to the default Slide Sorter view with six slides.

CHANGING TO SLIDE SHOW VIEW

You can use your computer screen to practice your slide show or to run a slide show. You'll learn more about computer slide shows in Chapter 16. In this section, you will learn how to switch in and out of Slide Show view.

1. **Click** on **slide 1**.

2. **Click** on the **Slide Show button**, which is the fifth button from the left. Your screen will go blank for a few seconds. Then the slide Show view will appear, showing slide 1.

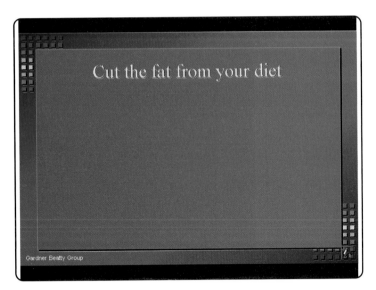

3. **Press** the **Esc key** on your keyboard. You will be returned to the Slide Sorter view.

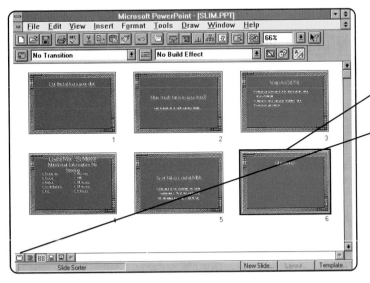

CHANGING TO SLIDE VIEW

1. **Click** on **slide 6**.

2. **Click** on the **Slide View button**. Slide 6 will appear in the Slide View format.

Changing the Size of the Slide in Slide View

You can enlarge the slide that you see in Slide View.

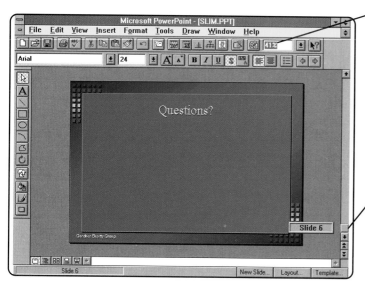

1. Click twice in the **Zoom Control box**. The 41% will be highlighted.

2. **Type 45** and **press Enter**. The slide will be enlarged.

Moving Around in Slide View

1. Place the **mouse arrow** on the scroll button. Then **press and hold** the mouse button. Notice that the current slide number appears to the left.

2. **Drag** the **scroll button** up and down the scroll bar and release the button when the number of the slide you want to see appears in the box. Then **drag** the **scroll button** back down to slide 6.

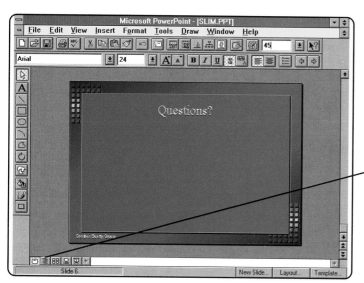

CHANGING TO OUTLINE VIEW

1. Click on the **Outline View button**, which is the second from the left at the bottom of your screen. The Outline view will appear.

Notice that you are at the bottom of the outline because slide 6 is still the selected slide.

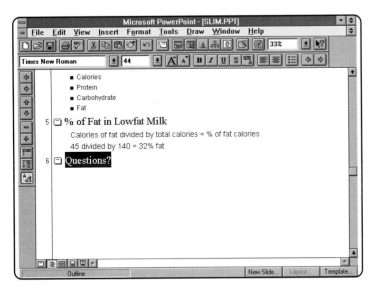

Also, notice on slide 4 that the Outline view shows only the left-hand bulleted list. (Strange, but Microsoft says that this is the way it is.) If you want to edit the right-hand bulleted list, you can do it in Slide view.

2. **Press** the **Page Up key** to move to the top of the outline.

3. **Click** on the **Save button** to save your work.

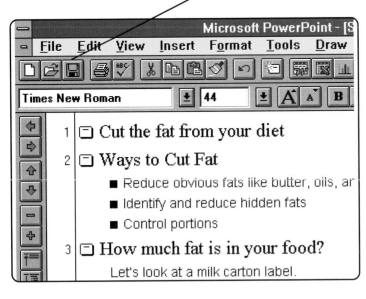

Editing and Styling Text

You can edit and style text in both the Slide and Outline views. Anything you can do to text in a word-processing program, you can do in PowerPoint. Additional styling features are discussed in Chapter 6. In this chapter you will do the following:

❖ Edit bullets in Outline view

❖ Change the case

❖ Add periods

❖ Delete bullets in Slide view

EDITING TEXT IN OUTLINE VIEW

1. **Open slim.ppt** if it is not already open. If you are not already in Outline view, see the section "Changing to Outline View" in Chapter 4. In this section, you will change the bullets on the second slide to checkmarks. You can also do this in Slide view.

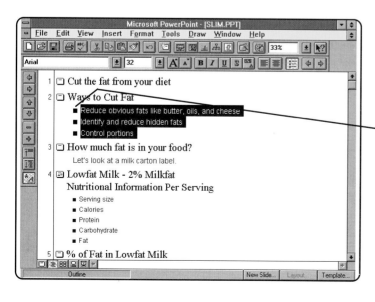

Changing Bullets to Checkmarks

1. **Click** to the **left of "Reduce"** and **drag** the highlight bar to the **end of "Control portions."**

2. **Release** the mouse button.

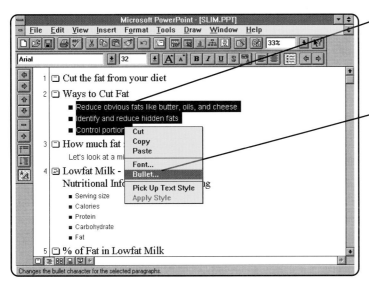

3. Keep the cursor on the highlighted text **and click** the **right mouse button**. A *quick* menu will appear.

4. Click on **Bullet**. The Bullet dialog box will appear.

Notice that the font is Monotype Sorts.

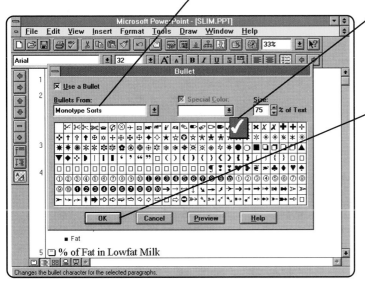

5. Click on the **bold checkmark** in the top row, eighth from the right. The checkmark will be enlarged.

6. Click on **OK**. The dialog box will disappear, and the bullets will be changed to checkmarks.

Switching to Slide View

1. Click on the **small slide** to the **right of number 1** to highlight the text in slide 1. As you place the cursor on the slide icon, the cursor will change to a four-headed arrow.

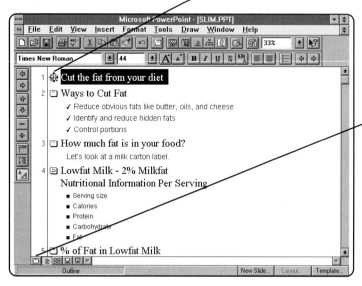

2. Click on the **Slide View button**, which is the first button at the bottom of your screen. The Slide View screen will appear, showing slide 1.

CHANGING THE CASE

You can change the capitalization of text to all uppercase or all lowercase or use a feature that puts in the correct capitalization for a title. In this section, you will correct the capitalization on the title slide.

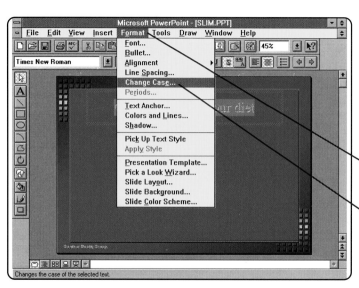

1. Click and drag the I-beam cursor **over the text** on slide 1 to highlight it.

2. Click on **Format**. A pulldown menu will appear.

3. Click on **Change Case**. The Change Case dialog box will appear.

4. **Click** on **Title Case** to place a dot in the circle.

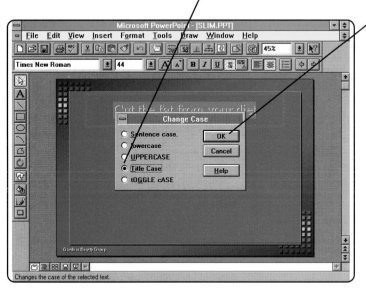

5. **Click** on **OK**. Slide 1 will appear with the title slide capitalized.

6. **Click anywhere** to remove the highlighting.

MAKING TEXT BOLD

Before you can format text, you must first highlight, or select, it.

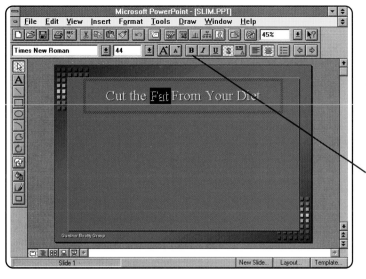

1. **Click** to the left of the word "Fat." The mouse pointer changes to an I-beam when it is in a text block.

2. **Drag** the I-beam **over** the word **"Fat"** to highlight it.

3. **Click** on the **Bold button**.

4. **Click outside** the **text block** to remove the highlighting and "deselect" the text block.

ADDING PERIODS TO TEXT

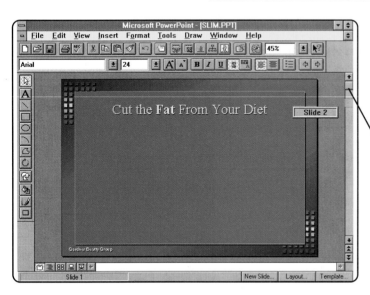

It's easy to be inconsistent in the use of periods on slides. Use the Periods feature to solve that problem.

1. Move the mouse arrow to the **scroll button**.

2. Press and **hold** the mouse button as you **drag** the **scroll button** down. When the slide 2 indicator appears, **release** the **mouse button**. Slide 2 will appear.

3. Click and **drag** the I-beam cursor **over the checkmarked text** to highlight it.

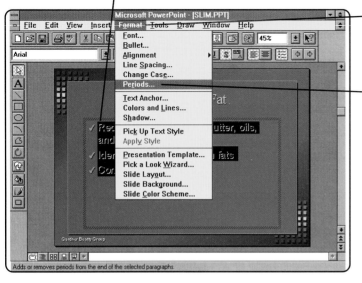

4. Click on **Format** in the menu bar. A pull-down menu will appear.

5. Click on **Periods**. The Periods dialog box will appear.

6. Click on **Add Periods** to place a dot in the circle if it is not already there.

7. Click on **OK**. Slide 2 will appear with the added periods.

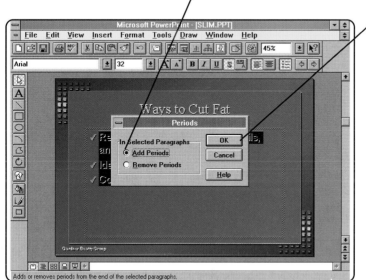

CHANGING TEXT SIZE

You change the text, or font, size just as you do in word processing programs.

1. Press the **Page Down key** on the keyboard two times to move to **slide 4**. This is another way to move around in Slide view.

2. Click to the left of **"Nutritional Information Per Serving"** and **drag** the **I-beam** over the text to highlight it.

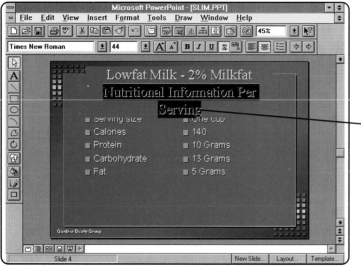

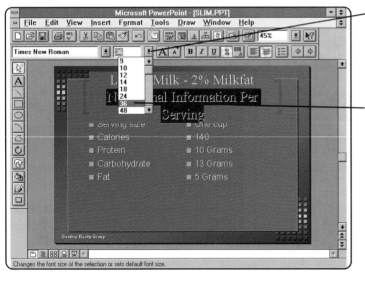

3. **Click** on the ⬇ to the **right** of the Font Size box. A drop-down menu will appear.

4. **Click** on **36**. The highlighted text will be resized to 36 points.

5. **Click anywhere outside** the **text block** to remove the highlighting and "deselect" the text block.

DELETING BULLETS

There are two ways you can delete bullets.

Deleting Bullets with the Format Menu

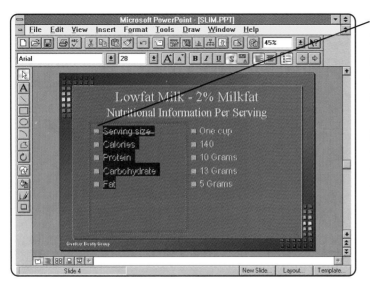

1. **Click** on the **text** in the **left text block**. A box will surround the text to show that the text block is selected.

2. **Click** to the **left** of **"Serving Size"** and **drag** the I-beam to the **end of "Fat"** to highlight the list.

3. **Click** on **Format** in the menu bar. A pull-down menu will appear.

4. **Click** on **Bullet**. The Bullet dialog box will appear.

5. **Click** on **Use a Bullet** to *remove* the ✕ from the box.

6. **Click** on **OK**. The bullets will be removed from the list.

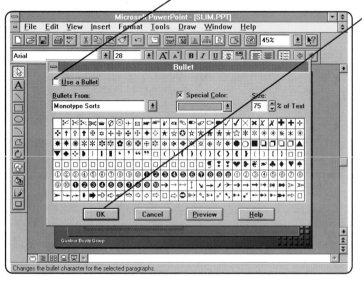

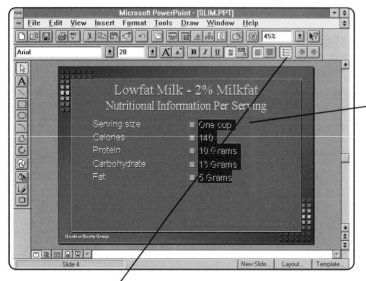

Deleting Bullets with the Bullet Button

1. Click on the **text** in the **right text block**. A box will surround the text to show that the text block is selected.

2. Click to the **left** of **"One cup"** and **drag** the I-beam to the **end of "5 Grams"** to highlight the list.

Notice that the Bullet button is lighter in color and looks pressed in to show that the highlighted text has bullets.

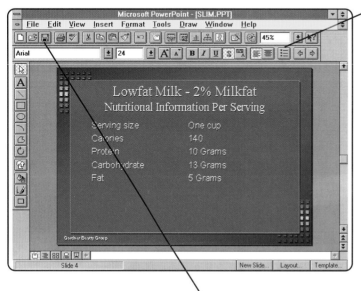

3. Click on the **Bullet button** in the toolbar. The bullets will disappear, and the Bullet button will no longer be pressed in and lighter in color.

If you want to add bullets, the steps are exactly the same.

4. Click anywhere outside the **text block** to remove the highlighting and "deselect" the text block.

5. Click on the **Save** button.

Working with Text Blocks

In PowerPoint, text is contained in a space called a text block. You can have multiple text blocks on a single slide. Each text block can be formatted and moved independently of other text blocks. *Placement guides* help align and center text blocks. This feature gives you tremendous control over the layout of your slide. In this chapter you will do the following:

❖ Add placement guides

❖ Move and resize text blocks

❖ Add a text block to a slide

❖ Color, shadow, and realign text

ADDING PLACEMENT GUIDES

You can move text anywhere on a slide by moving the text block that holds the text. In this section, you will add placement guides to help with exact positioning.

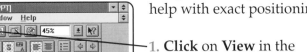
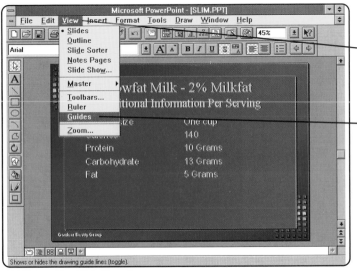

1. **Click** on **View** in the menu bar. A drop-down menu will appear.

2. **Click** on **Guides**. Dotted guide lines will appear at the vertical and horizontal centers of the slide.

CENTERING TEXT BLOCKS

To center a text block you must physically move the block to the center of the slide.

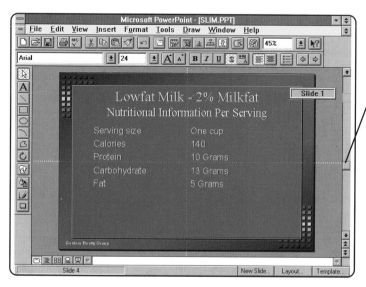

Centering the Slide 1 Text Block

1. **Move** the mouse arrow to the scroll button.

2. **Press and hold** the mouse button as you **drag** the scroll button to the **top** of the **scroll** bar.

3. **Release** the mouse button. Slide 1 will be on your screen.

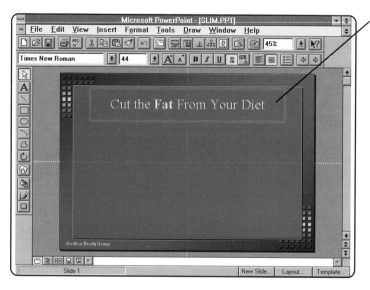

4. **Click anywhere** on the **text**. A box will surround the text and show the size and position of the text block.

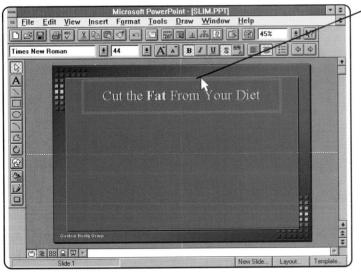

5. **Place** the I-beam cursor on the border of the **text block**, *but not on the center guide*. The cursor will become an arrow. You may have to fiddle with the placement of the cursor to get it to change into an arrow.

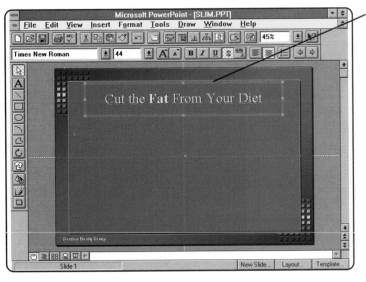

6. **Press and hold** the mouse button. Solid squares, or handles, will appear on the border of the text block. A dotted-line box will surround the text. Another dotted line box will appear just inside the text block border. Before you go to the next step, make certain that the mouse arrow is not on one of the handles.

7. **Drag** the cursor **down** to the **horizontal guide line**. As you drag, the dotted outlines of the text and the text block will move with the cursor. When the middle of the text is close to the center guide, it will "jump" into place. Magic! Placement guide lines act like a magnet pulling the text block into place automatically.

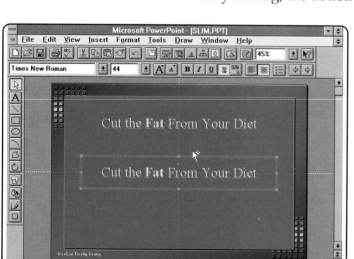

8. **Release** the mouse button. The text will be centered on the slide.

Centering the Slide 6 Text Block

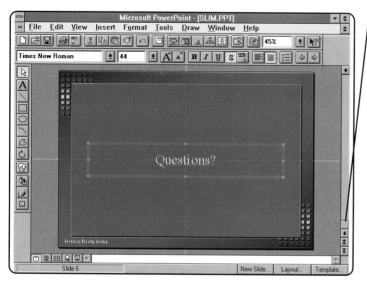

1. **Place** the mouse arrow on the **scroll button**.

2. **Press and hold** the mouse button as you **drag** the scroll button to the **bottom** of the **scroll bar**.

3. **Release** the mouse button. Slide 6 will be on your screen.

4. **Repeat steps 4 through 8** in the previous section to center the "Questions?" text block in slide 6.

RESIZING TEXT BLOCKS

In this section, you will make the bulleted list text blocks on slide 4 smaller so you can add text later to the bottom of the slide.

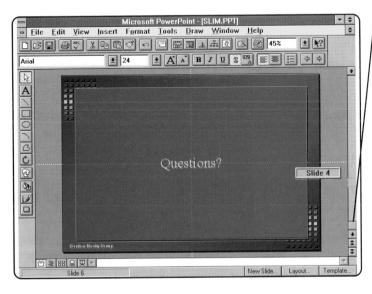

1. **Place** the mouse arrow on the **scroll button**.

2. **Press and hold** the mouse button as you **drag** the scroll button **up** until **slide 4** appears to the left of the scroll bar.

3. **Release** the mouse button. Slide 4 will be on your screen.

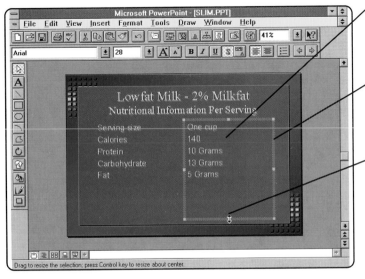

4. **Click** on the **right-hand text block** to select it if it is not already selected.

5. **Click** on the **border** of the **text block**. Handles will appear on the border.

6. **Place** the **cursor** on the **bottom middle handle**. The cursor will become a double-headed arrow.

7. **Press and hold** the mouse button. The double-headed arrow will become a plus sign.

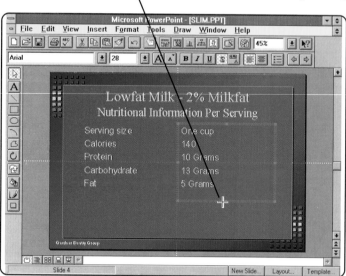

8. **Drag** the **plus sign** to just **below** the last word in the list. **Release** the mouse button. It's okay if it seems to "stick" as you drag up. Simply continue to press and hold the mouse button as you drag the line up to where you want it.

9. **Repeat steps 4 through 8** to resize the left-hand text block.

ALIGNING TEXT WITHIN A BLOCK

In this example, you will right-align text so that it lines up on the last letter in each line.

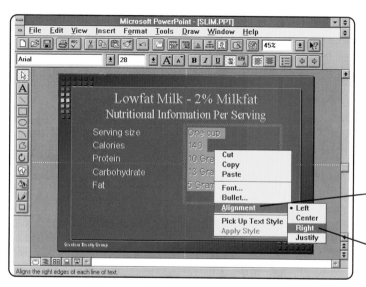

1. **Click** to the **left** of "One cup" and drag the I-beam cursor to the bottom of the list. The text will be highlighted.

2. **Click** the **right mouse button**. A text edit menu will appear.

3. **Click** on **Alignment**. A second menu will appear.

4. **Click** on **Right**. The text will appear aligned to the right.

USING GUIDES WHEN MOVING AND ALIGNING TEXT BLOCKS

In the previous section, you aligned text within a text block. You can also move and align text blocks themselves. When you do this, guides can help with the exact placement of a text block. In the following sections, you will move the vertical guide and then use it as a placement guide for a text block.

Moving Guides to Help with Alignment

Guides can do more than show the center of the slide. A guide can be moved to an exact spot and then used as a placement guide.

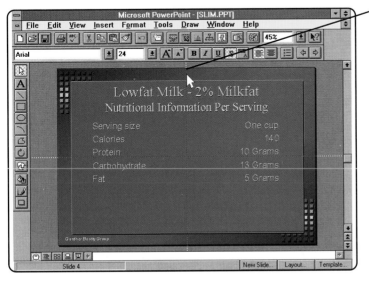

1. **Move** the **cursor** to the **top outside frame** of the slide. It will become an arrow. (**Note**: If you move the cursor inside the text block, it will turn into an I-beam. In that case, it won't let you click on the vertical guide in step 2 below.)

2. **Place the arrow** on the **vertical guide line** and **press and hold** the mouse button. The arrow will change to a white box with numbers inside.

When the guide is at the center, the number is 0.00. As you move the guide line, the number changes, showing how many inches away from center you have moved.

3. **Drag** the **guide line** to the **left** until the number **3.75** shows in the box Then **release** the mouse button.

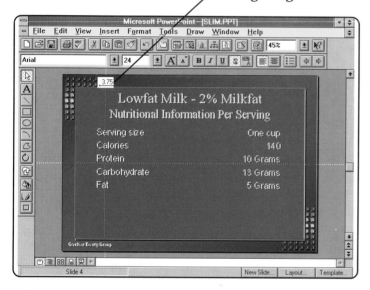

Aligning a Text Block with a Guide

1. **Press and hold** the **Shift key** and **click** on the **left-hand text block**. This is a shortcut way to select the text block and make handles appear.

2. **Click and hold anywhere** on the **border** *except on a handle box*, and **drag** the **block** to the **right**, until the left-hand edge "jumps" to the guide line. Notice that the *inside edge of the shaded text block border* snaps to the guide line. You will need to take that into account when trying to align text.

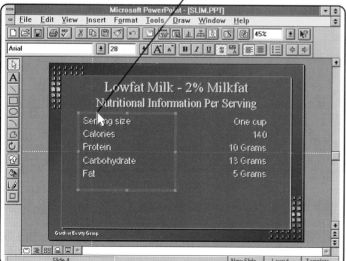

3. **Release** the mouse. **Click** on the **slide background** to deselect the text box.

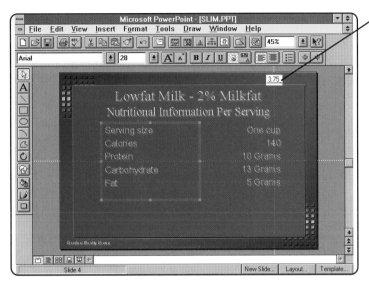

4. Repeat steps 1 through 3 in the "Moving Guides to Help with alignment" section to **move** the **vertical guide line right** to **3.75**

5. Press and hold the **Shift key** and **click** on the **right-hand text block** to show the selection border and handles.

6. Click anywhere on the **border** *except on a handle box*, and **hold and drag** the **block** to the **left** until the edge "jumps" to the guide line.

7. Release the mouse button.

Aligning Two Text Blocks with Each Other

In this section, you will align the tops of the two text

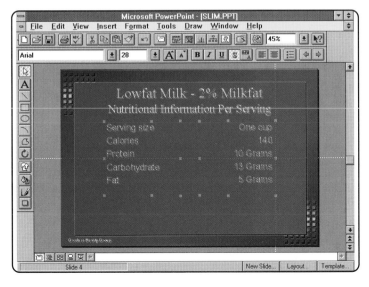

blocks you just moved so that the text in the left block is perfectly aligned with the text in the right block.

1. Press and hold the **Shift key** and **click** on the **right text block** if it is not already selected.

2. Press and hold the **shift key** and **click** on the **left text block**. This will select *both* of the text blocks at the same time. You will see a border of handles.

3. Click on **Draw** in the menu bar. A pull-down menu will appear.

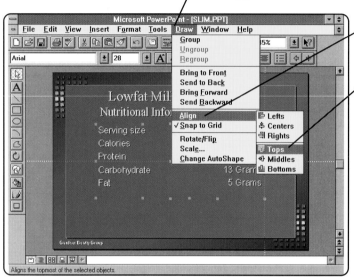

4. Click on **Align.** A second menu will appear.

5. Click on **Tops**. The tops of the selected text boxes will now be evenly aligned.

ADDING A TEXT BLOCK

You add text to an existing text block by simply typing the additional text. In this section, you will add text outside of an existing text block. This requires you to use the Text tool to create another text block. First, you will move the guides to help you align the new text block with existing text.

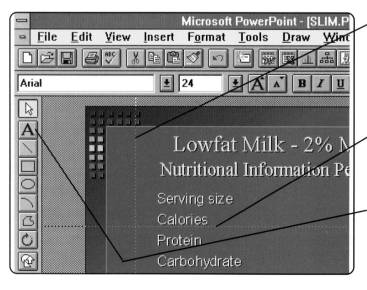

1. Move the **vertical guide left** to **4.25**. See "Adding Placement Guides" earlier in this chapter if you need help.

2. Move the **horizontal guide up** to just **below Calories**.

3. Click on the **Text tool**.

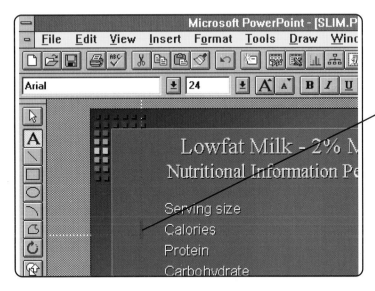

4. **Move** the **cursor on to the slide**. It will become a vertical line with a crossbar at the bottom.

5. **Place** the **cursor** on **top** of the **vertical guide line** and **place** the **crossbar on** the **horizontal guide line** to the **left** of the word **"Calories."**

6. **Click** to set the cursor. A small, empty text block will appear.

7. **Type #1**. You have now created a text block containing text. In the next section, you will color and add a shadow to this text.

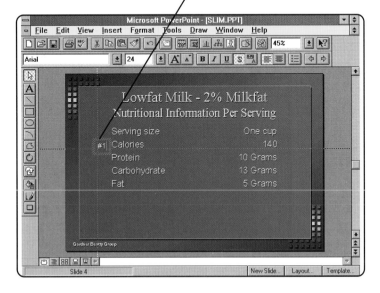

COLORING TEXT AND ADDING A SHADOW

1. **Drag** the I-beam **over "#1"** to highlight it.

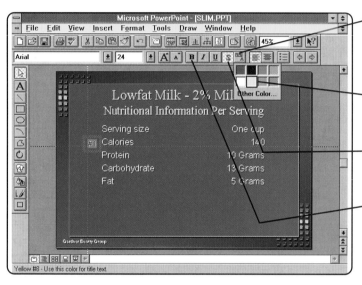

2. **Click** on the **Text Color button**. A color menu will appear in the toolbar.

3. **Click** on the **yellow square**.

4. **Click** on the **Text Shadow button** (the S).

5. **Click** on the **Bold button**.

6. **Click off** the **text block** so that you can see the text.

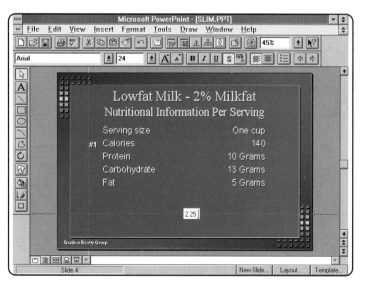

COPYING A TEXT BLOCK WITH DRAG AND DROP

1. **Move** the **horizontal guide down** to **2.25**. See "Moving Guides to Help with alignment" if you need help.

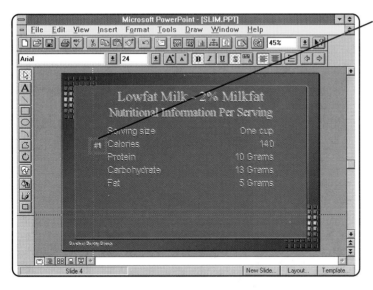

2. Click on **#1**. The text block will appear around the text.

3. Press and hold the **Ctrl key**.

4. Move the **arrow** onto the border of the text block until a small cross appears beside the arrow.

5. Continue to **hold** the **Ctrl key**. **Press and hold** the mouse button and **drag** the **mouse pointer down** to the guide lines. As you drag, keep the mouse pointer inside the vertical guide line. An outline of the text block will "jump" to the guide lines as shown in this example.

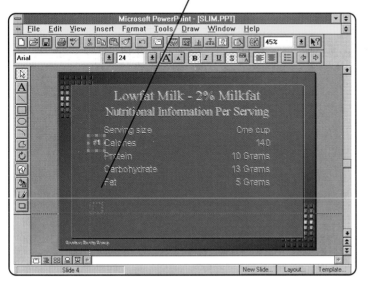

6. Release the **mouse button first**. Then **release** the **Ctrl key**. Notice that the inside edges of the text block border are aligned with the guide lines.

ADDING TEXT TO A TEXT BLOCK

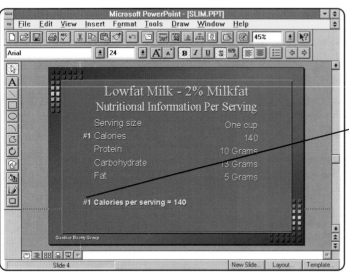

Now that you have a text block at the bottom of the slide, you can add text to it by simply typing it in the block.

1. Place the cursor **after** the **#1** in the text block.

2. Press the **spacebar** and **type Calories per serving = 140**.

CENTERING TEXT AND A TEXT BLOCK

Because this new text block is not part of the predesigned slide, it does not contain any formatting commands. You have to provide them. In this section, you will center the text within the text block then center the text block on the slide.

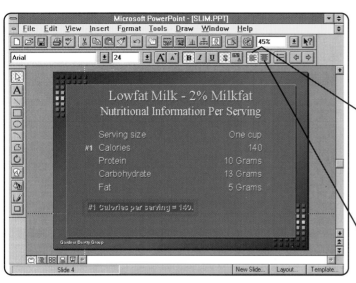

1. Drag the I-beam cursor **over** the **text** to select it. Notice that the Left Alignment button in the toolbar is pressed in to show that this text is left-aligned.

2. Click on the **Center button**.

3. **Move** the **vertical guide line** to **0.00**.

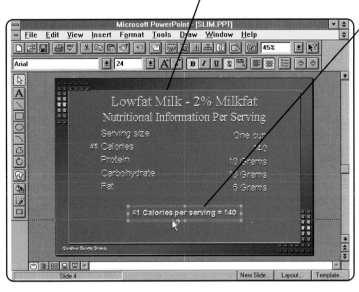

4. With the cursor as an arrow, **click** on the border of the **text block** to see the selection handles.

5. **Click and hold** on the **text border**, *not a handle*, and **drag** the **text box** toward the middle guide line until it "jumps" to center. When you **release** the mouse button, the center handles should be aligned with the vertical guide.

COLORING A TEXT BLOCK

Previously in this chapter, you colored text. In this section, you will color the text block itself and put a colored line around the text block.

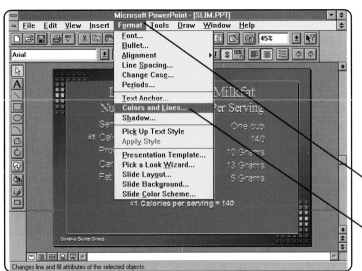

Adding Fill to a Text Block

1. **Press and hold** the **shift key** and **click** on the **Calories per Serving text block** to show handles if it is not already selected.

2. **Click** on **Format** in the menu bar.

3. **Click** on **Colors and Lines**. The Colors and Lines dialog box will appear.

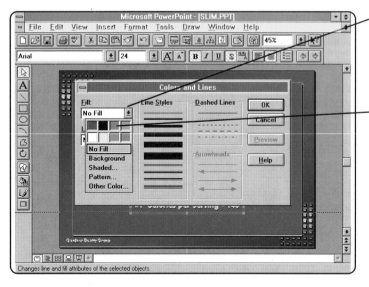

4. Click on the ⬇ to the **right** of **No Fill**. A drop-down color menu will appear.

5. Click on the **dark pink square** (third from the left on the top row). The drop-down menu will disappear and the Fill box will be pink.

Adding a Line Around a Text Block

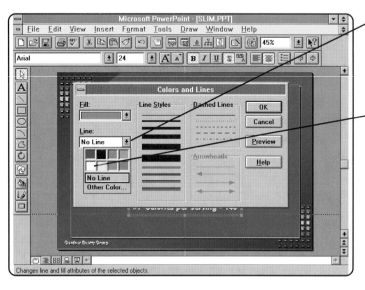

1. Click on the ⬇ to the **right** of **No Line**. A drop-down color menu will appear.

2. Click on the **white square**. The drop-down menu will disappear.

3. Click on **OK**.

4. Click off the **text block** to see what it looks like.

REMOVING PLACEMENT GUIDES

1. Click on **View** in the menu bar. A pull-down menu will appear.

2. Click on **Guides** to remove the ✔.

Notice that the placement guides are no longer visible on the slides.

SAVING THE PRESENTATION

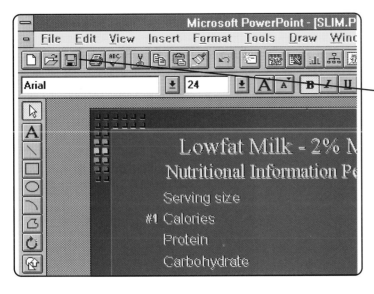

1. Click on the **Save button** in the toolbar to save your work.

Printing a Paper Copy

PowerPoint uses standard Windows-based commands to print. PowerPoint will print colors as shades of gray unless you have a color printer. Even with a very fast printer, it will take forever to print your slides if you have used a color template. Depending on the predesigned template you have chosen, the printed copies may be difficult to read because gray does not show the differences in color. You can, however, choose to print all background colors and fill in white and all text and lines in black. This makes for much faster printing. In this chapter you will do the following:

❖ Print colored copies of your slides
❖ Eliminate background shading and print in pure black and white

PRINTING COLORED COPIES

In this example, you will print colored copies of the slides you created in Chapters 1 through 5. If you do

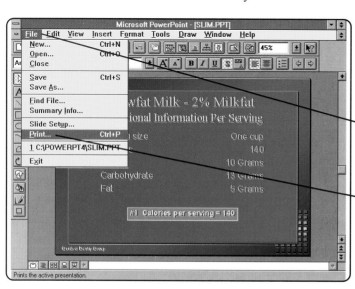

not have a color printer, skip step 3 in this section and go to step 1 in the next section, entitled "Printing in Pure Black and White."

1. **Click** on **File** on the menu bar. A pull-down menu will appear.

2. **Click** on **Print**. The Printing dialog box will appear.

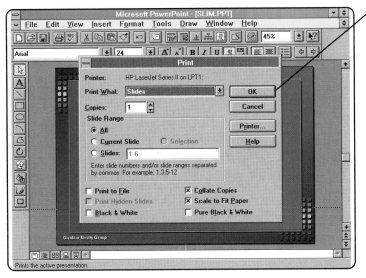

3. Click on **OK**. One set of all of your slides will be printed in color. You will have a considerable hour-glass intermission because printing in color takes a long time. If you don't have a color printer, your printer will print in shades of gray, which takes a long time. In addition, the background can make the printed copies hard to read. We recommend you use the option described below when you print paper copies of your slides

PRINTING IN PURE BLACK AND WHITE

The option to print in pure black and white eliminates background colors. It is useful in printing drafts and crisp, clear copies of notes and handout pages.

1. Repeat steps 1 and 2 above to open the Print dialog box.

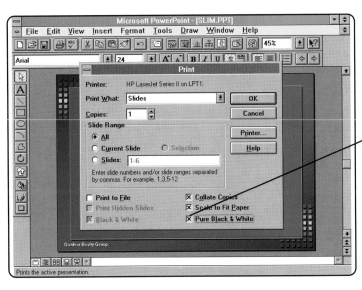

2. Click on **Pure Black & White** to insert an ✕ in the box. This will eliminate all background colors and print text and lines in black. This affects only the printed copy. It has no effect on the original slides.

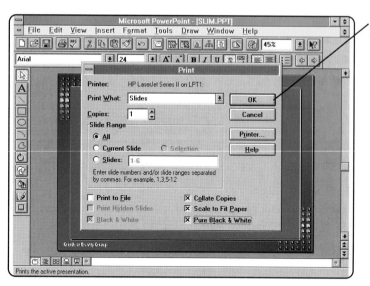

3. **Click** on **OK**. Full-page black-and-white copies of all of the slides will be printed.

PRINTING OPTIONS: MULTIPLE COPIES AND SELECTED PAGES

You can click on the ▲ or ▼ to indicate the number of copies to be printed. In the example above, you printed one copy of each slide.

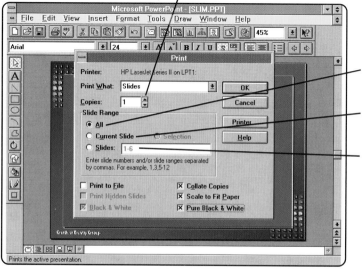

You have three options for printing selected pages:

❖ Printing all slides (which is currently selected)

❖ Printing the currently selected slide

❖ Printing a range such as 1,3,5-6. This means that you want to print pages 1 and 3, and 5 to 6.

Producing Slides Through a Service Bureau

After you've designed your presentation, the next step is to produce it. Most people don't produce slides themselves. You can send your PowerPoint file to a service bureau and it will produce them for you (overnight, if you like). PowerPoint includes a special printer driver for sending your file to Genigraphics, a leading service bureau. However, there are numerous other high-quality service bureaus nationwide, such as Elegant Digital Imaging, Inc., in Steamboat Springs, Colorado. Most bureaus will take your PowerPoint file without a special driver. The choice of bureaus is yours. In this chapter you will do the following:

❖ Learn how to send a file to Genigraphics

❖ Learn how to send a file to other service bureaus

SENDING A FILE TO GENIGRAPHICS

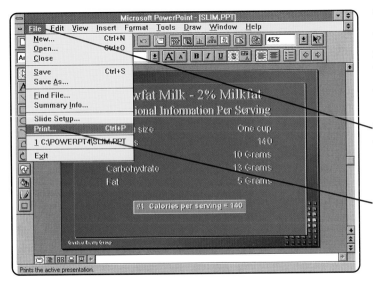

To send your slides directly to Genigraphics, you must first open the Print dialog box so that you can use their special printer driver.

1. **Click** on **File** in the menu bar. A pull-down menu will appear.

2. **Click** on **Print**. The Print dialog box will appear.

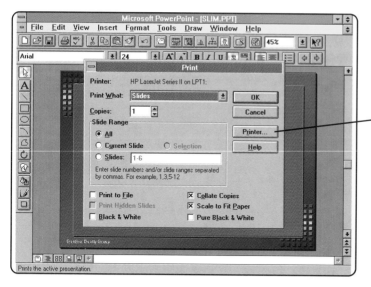

Specifying Genigraphics as the Printer

1. Click on **Printer**. The Print Setup dialog box will appear.

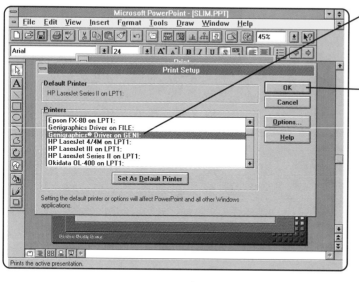

2. Click on **Genigraphics Driver on GENI** to highlight it.

3. Click on **OK**. The Print Setup dialog box will close. The Print dialog box will reappear.

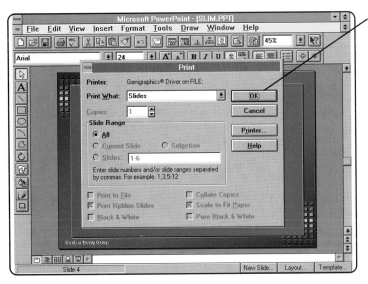

4. Click on **OK**. A Printing message box will appear briefly. Next, the Genigraphics Job Instructions dialog box will appear.

Specifying the Output Medium

You can have your presentation produced in one (or more) of four mediums:

❖ 35mm slides with plastic mounts

❖ 35mm slides with glass mounts

❖ 8" x 10" overheads

❖ 8" x 10" prints

The standard (default) setting is one set of 35mm slides with plastic mounts. To select one or more mediums, follow these steps:

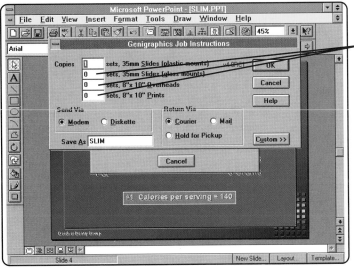

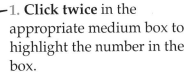

1. Click twice in the appropriate medium box to highlight the number in the box.

2. Type the **number of copies** you want.

3. Repeat steps 1 and 2 for each type of medium you want produced.

Telling Genigraphics
How to Return the Slides

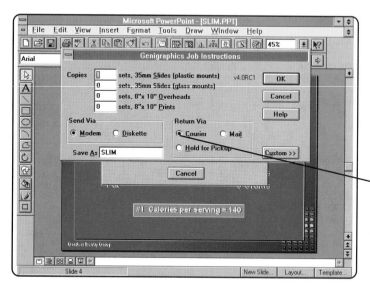

Genigraphics can return your slides to you three ways:

❖ Courier

❖ Mail

❖ Hold for Pickup

1. **Click** on the appropriate **choice** in the Return Via box to insert a dot in the circle. In this example, **click** on **Courier**.

Sending Your
Presentation on Diskette

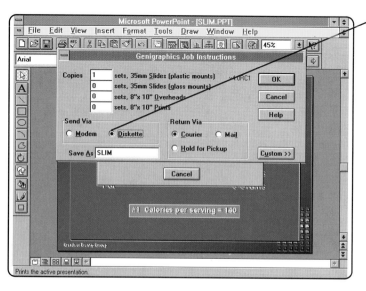

1. **Click** on **Diskette** to put a dot in the circle if one is not already there.

Notice you can also send your presentation via modem, if you have one.

Customizing Print Instructions

You can add customized instructions and a rush order request in the Job Instructions dialog box. You should discuss these instructions with your local Genigraphics office before including them.

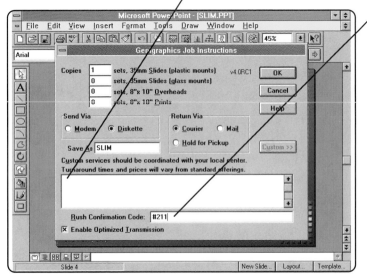

1. **Click** on the **Custom button** in the Job Instructions dialog box. The box will expand at the bottom to include two test boxes for typing the special instructions and a rush order confirmation code.

2. **Click** in the **Custom box** and **type** the **instructions** you want to include with you file.

3. If you have received a Rush confirmation code from Genigraphics, **click in the Rush confirmation code box** and **type** the **confirmation number**.

4. **Click** on **OK**. The Save As dialog box will appear.

Specifying the Diskette Location

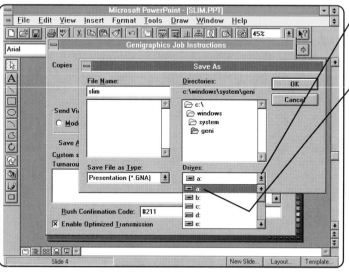

1. Click on the ⬇ to the right of the Drives list box. A drop-down list will appear.

2. Click on **a:** (or **b:**). The drop-down list will disappear and a: (or b:) will be in the list box.

3. Insert a blank, formatted, **diskette** in drive a: (or b:).

4. Click on **OK**. After a brief printing intermission, the Genigraphics Billing Information dialog box will appear.

Entering Billing and Shipping Information

1. Press the **Tab key** and **type** your **billing information**, **shipping choice**, and **tax information** (if required) in the appropriate text boxes.

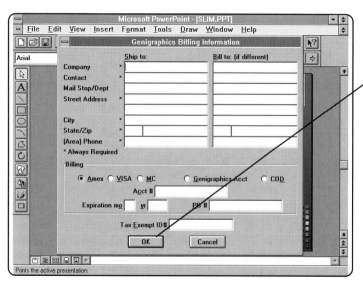

2. Click on **OK**. After a brief printing intermission, a Genigraphics dialog box will appear, saying that your slides have been saved to file.

3. Click on **OK** on the dialog box to close the box. The slides are ready to be sent to production.

Changing the Printer Driver

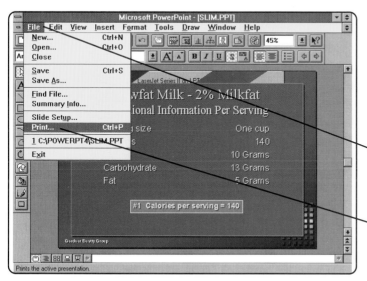

After you have saved your slide presentation to a diskette, it is important to remember to change the printer driver back to your standard driver.

1. Click on **File** in the menu bar. A pull-down menu will appear.

2. Click on **Print**. The Print dialog box will appear.

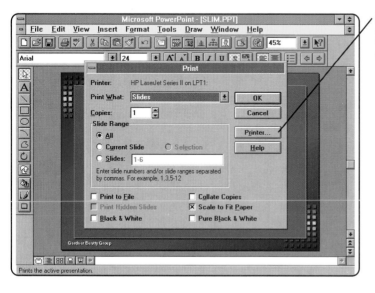

3. Click on **Printer**. The Printer Setup dialog box will appear.

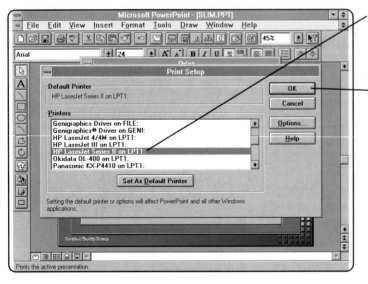

4. Click on your **standard printer driver** to highlight it.

5. Click on **OK**. The Print dialog box will reappear.

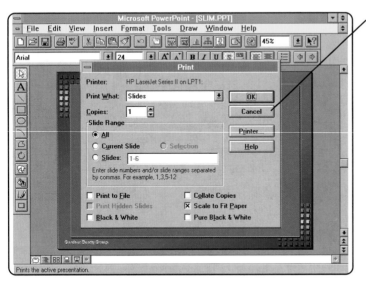

6. Click on **Cancel**. Your standard printer driver is now reinstalled.

SENDING A FILE TO OTHER SERVICE BUREAUS

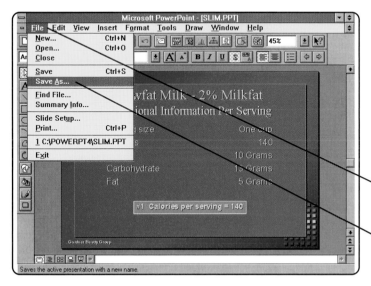

You are not limited to using only one service bureau. Feel free to call other bureaus to shop prices. Many bureaus require only that you send them your PowerPoint file on a diskette. They do the rest!

1. **Click** on **File**. A pull-down menu will appear.

2. **Click** on **Save As**. The Save As dialog box will appear.

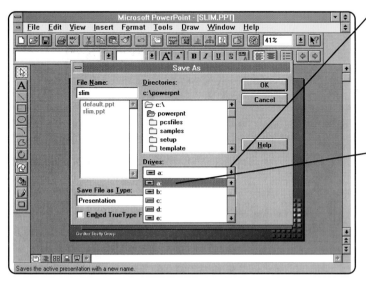

3. **Click** on the ↓ to the right of the drives list box. A drop-down list will appear.

4. **Insert** a blank, formatted **diskette** in drive a: (or b:).

5. **Click** on **a:** (or b:). The drop-down list will disappear and a: (or b:) will be in the list box.

6. **Click** on **OK**. After a brief hourglass intermission, the Summary Information dialog box will appear.

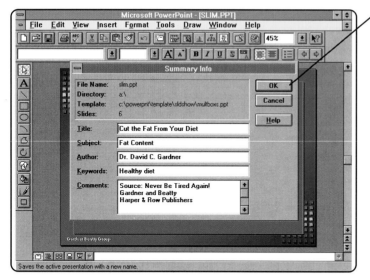

7. Click on **OK**.
Congratulations! Your slides are now saved to a diskette and ready to be sent to the service bureau of your choice.

Creating and Printing Notes and Handouts

A notes page shows a slide in the top half of the page and keeps the bottom half of the page free for text. You can print notes pages for the speaker and different notes pages for the audience. The master page for notes can be modified to have a larger font size. You can also print handout pages that contain from two to six slides per page. In this chapter you will do the following:

❖ Create and print a page with speaker's notes

❖ Change the master page for notes and create and print audience notes pages

❖ Print handout pages

CREATING SPEAKER'S NOTES

Speaker's notes can be anything from special comments the speaker wants to make about the contents of the slide to reminders to perform some specific action, such as handing out supplementary material. In this section, you will create a note for slide 4.

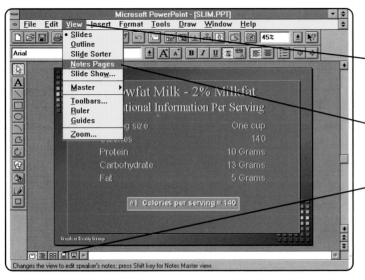

1. **Go to slide 4** if you are not already there.

2. **Click** on **View** in the menu bar. A pull-down menu will appear.

3. **Click** on **Notes Pages**. Slide 4 will appear in Notes Pages view.

(You can also click on the Notes Pages View button at the bottom of the screen rather than use the pull-down menu.)

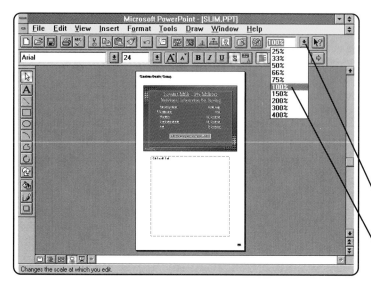

Magnifying the Notes Section

This is a bird's-eye view of the Notes page. You need to zoom in for a magnified view in order to work in the Notes section.

1. Click on ↧ to the **right** of the **zoom control box**.

2. Click on **100%**. The Notes Pages view will be magnified.

INCREASING FONT SIZE ON THE NOTES MASTER PAGE

The Notes section is set up to have a 12-point Arial font. It's much easier for the speaker to read the notes if they are in a larger font. In this section, you will change the notes master page so that it has a larger font size. A *master page* is a template that controls the placement of type, the font, and the font size.

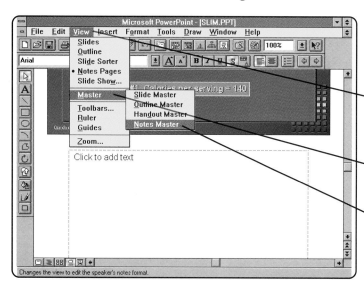

1. Click on **View** in the menu bar. A pull-down menu will appear.

2. Click on **Master**. A second menu will appear.

3. Click on **Notes Master**. The notes master page will appear, showing five style levels.

The Notes section is set up as an outline with each level of text at 12 points. In this example, you will change the font size to 18 points for the first level of the outline text. This will change every notes page.

1. **Click** to the **left** of the word **"Click"** in the notes text block at the bottom of the slide.

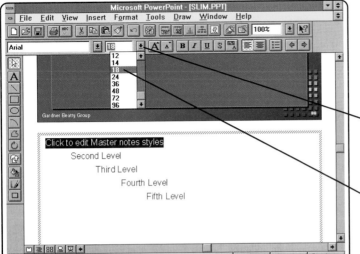

2. **Drag** the I-beam **over** the **first line of text** to highlight it.

3. **Click** on ⬇ to the right of the font size box. A drop-down list will appear.

4. **Click** on **18**. The highlighted text will change to 18 points.

Now you will switch back to Notes Pages view.

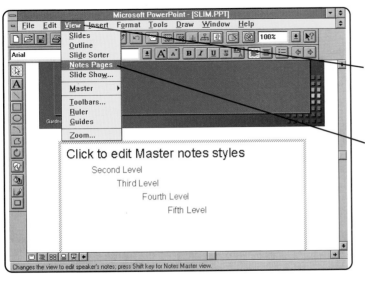

5. **Click** on **View** in the menu bar. A pull-down menu will appear.

6. **Click** on **Notes Pages**. The Notes Pages view for slide 4 will appear.

Adding Text to the Notes Section

1. Click on the **text block** on the **bottom** of the page if it is not already selected.

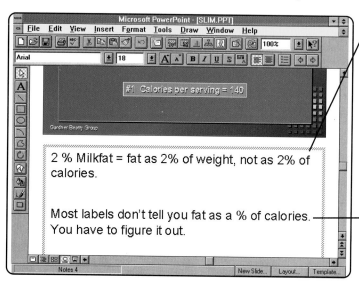

2. Type the following:

2% Milkfat = fat as 2% of weight, not as 2% of calories

3. Press Enter twice to put extra space between the notes and **type the following:**

Most labels don't tell you fat as a % of calories. You have to figure it out.

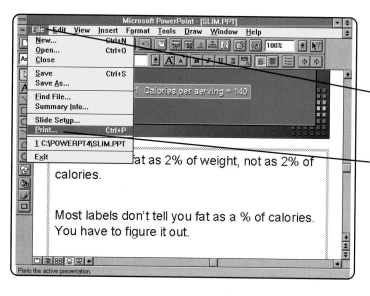

PRINTING A NOTES PAGE

1. Click on **File** in the menu bar. A pull-down menu will appear.

2. Click on **Print**. The Print dialog box will appear.

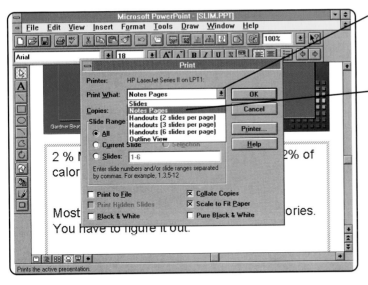

3. Click on ⬇ to the right of the Print What box. A drop-down list will appear.

4. Click on **Notes Pages**. It will replace the text in the box.

5. Click on **Current Slide** to print slide 4.

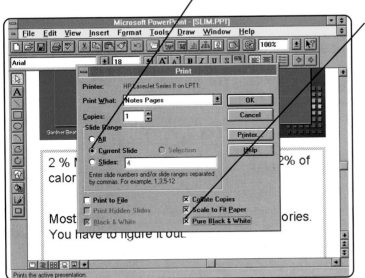

6. Click on **Pure Black & White** to put an ✕ in the box.

7. Click on **OK**. After a brief printing intermission, a notes page for slide 4 will print.

CREATING AND PRINTING NOTES PAGES FOR THE AUDIENCE

If you want to give your audience an impressive package that contains a copy of each slide and room to make notes, customize the notes pages with the following steps. If you have been following along with the examples in the book, do the steps in the following section. Otherwise, go directly to step 1 of "Adding a 'Notes' Header" on the next page.

Deleting the Speaker's Notes

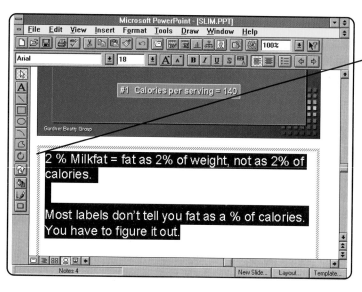

1. **Click** to the **left** of **2%**.

2. **Press and hold** the mouse button as you **drag** the I-beam **over** the **text** you typed in the notes section of slide 4 to highlight it.

3. **Release** the mouse button.

4. **Press** the **Delete key** to delete the text.

Adding a "Notes" Header

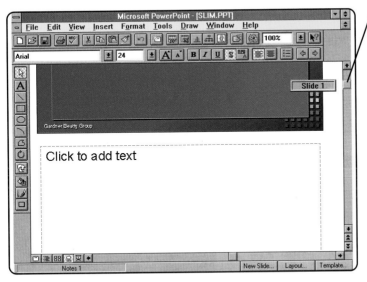

1. **Move** the mouse arrow to the **scroll button**.

2. **Press and hold** the mouse button as you **drag** the **scroll** button to the **top** of the **bar** to go to **slide 1**.

3. **Release** the mouse button. Slide 1 will appear.

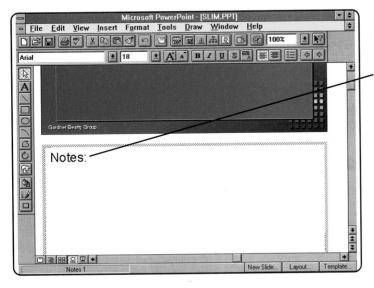

4. **Click inside** the **notes text block**.

5. **Type Notes:**. Notice that it appears in 18-point type.

Copying and Pasting Between Notes Pages

In this section, you will copy "Notes:" from page 1 and paste it into the remaining notes pages.

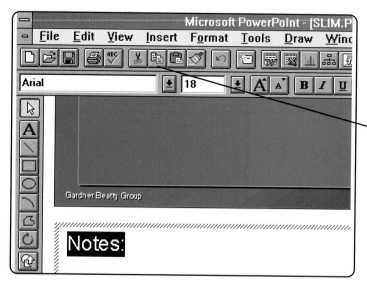

1. Press and hold the mouse button as you **drag** the I-beam **over Notes:** to highlight the word and the colon.

2. Click on the **Copy button** in the toolbar. The text will be copied to the Clipboard, a temporary storage area in your computer.

3. Press the **Page Down key** on your keyboard to move to slide 2.

4. Click inside the **text block** at the **bottom** of the **page** to set the cursor.

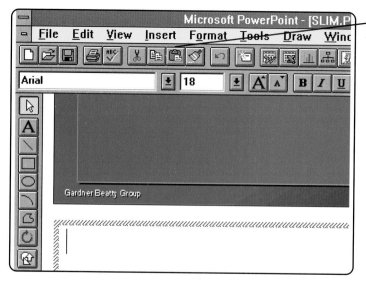

5. Click on the **Paste button** on the toolbar. "Notes:" will be pasted into the slide in an 18-point type size.

6. Repeat steps 3 through 5 to copy the text to slides 3 through 6. You don't have to copy the text again. You can continue to paste it on successive pages until it is replaced in the Clipboard by another copy or delete command.

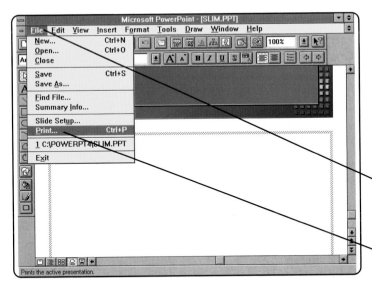

Printing Audience Notes

Printing copies of your slides with a note-taking area can be very useful for your audience.

1. **Click** on **File** in the menu bar. A pull-down menu will appear.

2. **Click** on **Print**. The Print dialog box will appear.

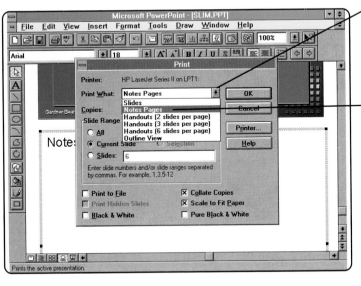

3. **Click** on the ⬇ to the **right** of the **Print What box**. A drop-down list will appear.

4. **Click** on **Notes Pages** to highlight it. It will replace the text in the box.

In addition, notice that you can print handouts. Handouts can be useful when you are designing your slides. You can see up to six slides per page, and they give you a good overview of your presentation.

5. **Click** on **All** to put a dot in the circle.

6. **Click** to **place** an ✕ in the **Pure Black & White box** if it is not already there.

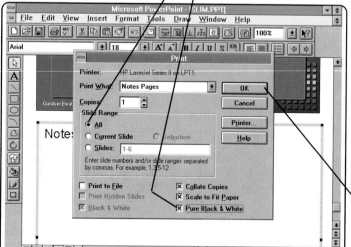

The Print dialog box remembers the selections that were in effect the last time you printed. Therefore, you need to check all the options to see if they are appropriate for your current print job.

7. **Click** on **OK**. The Print Status message box will appear briefly. The audience notes will be printed.

SAVING THE NOTES AND CHANGING THE VIEW

1. **Click** on the **Save button** to save your work.

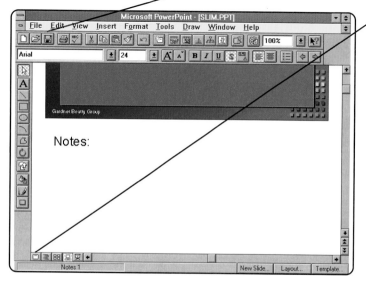

If you are planning to go on to Chapter 10, **click** on the **Slide View button** on the bottom of the slide.

Press and hold the mouse button as you **drag** the **scroll button** to the **top** of the **bar** to go to **slide 1**. Now you are ready to start the next chapter.

Program Manager

Part II: Creating a Customized Presentation

Drawing

PowerPoint has a very versatile drawing program that includes a number of predesigned shapes. You can layer text blocks and drawn items by sending one element to the back or bringing an element to the front. You can group layered elements so that they become one element and can be moved together. In this chapter you will do the following:

❖ Draw a rectangle

❖ Layer and group elements

❖ Duplicate a slide

❖ Edit and move a grouped element

❖ Change the shape of a text block

❖ Create Auto Shapes

DRAWING A RECTANGLE

Showing Guides

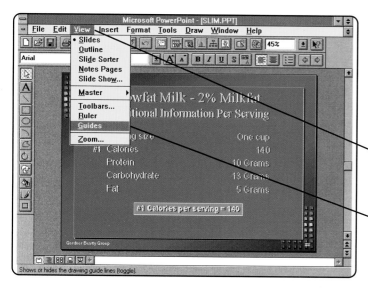

Unless you have an eagle eye (like our editor), use guides to help place drawn items.

1. **Open slim.ppt** to slide 4 if it is not already open.

2. **Click** on **View** in the menu bar. A pull-down menu will appear.

3. **Click** on **Guides**. Dotted lines will appear at the horizontal and vertical center of the slide.

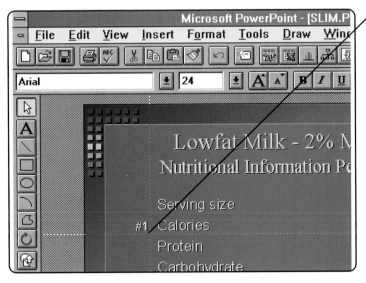

4. **Move** the **vertical and horizontal guides** so that they look like this example. On our computer, we placed the vertical guide at 3.75 to the left of center. The horizontal guide should be just under the word "Calories". Your numerical positions may be different, depending on your video driver. If you need help, see the section "Moving Guides to Help with alignment" in Chapter 6.

Zooming In for Close-Up Work

1. **Click** on **#1**. The text block will appear. This tells the Zoom Control where to focus when it zooms in.

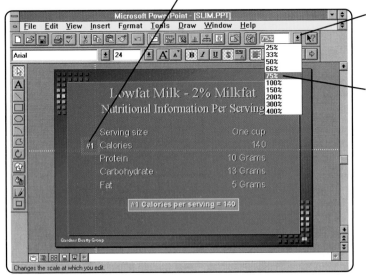

2. **Click** on ↓ to the **right** of the **zoom control box**. A drop-down list will appear.

3. **Click** on **75%**. The view will be magnified.

Drawing the Rectangle

In this section, you will use the Rectangle tool. Notice that there are many shapes from which to choose.

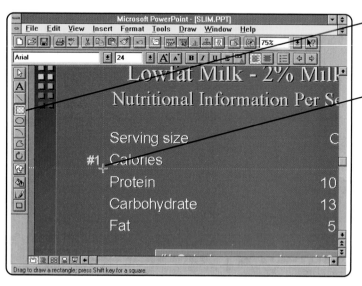

1. **Click** on the **Rectangle tool** in the Drawing toolbar at the left of your screen.

2. **Place** the cursor at the **intersection** of the **vertical and horizontal guides**. The cursor will be in the shape of a plus sign.

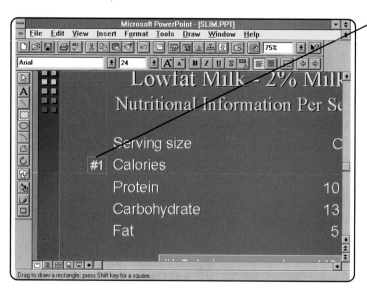

3. **Press and hold** the mouse button and **drag** the cursor **up and** to the **left**. A rectangle will form, like the one you see in this example. As long as you continue to hold the mouse button, you can fiddle with the size and shape of the rectangle.

4. **Release** the mouse button when the rectangle is the size and shape you see here.

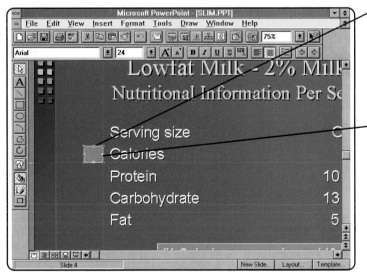

Notice that the rectangle appears with the fill color and line you selected the last time you used lines and fills in Chapter 6.

Notice also that the rectangle appears on top of the text block and completely blocks it from view. You'll fix that in the next section.

SENDING AN ELEMENT TO THE BACK

When you placed the rectangle over the #1 text block, PowerPoint automatically placed it on top. You can tell PowerPoint to place it behind the text.

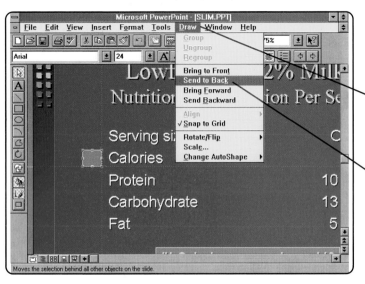

1. **Click** on the **rectangle** if it does not already have handles on it border.

2. **Click** on **Draw** in the menu bar. A pull-down menu will appear.

3. **Click** on **Send to Back**. The rectangle will be sent to the back, and the #1 text block will appear in the front.

DUPLICATING A SLIDE
WITH THE EDIT MENU

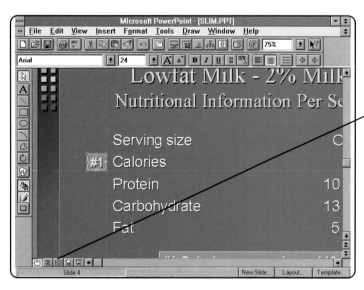

In this section, you will duplicate slide 4. First you have to change to Slide Sorter view.

1. **Click** on the **Slide Sorter View button** at the bottom of your screen.

The Slide Sorter view will appear.

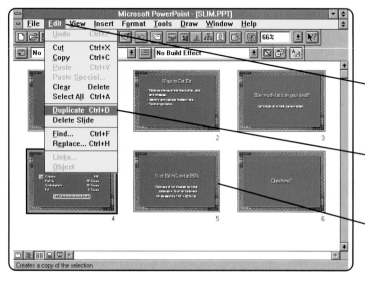

2. **Click** on **slide 4**. A selection border will appear around the slide.

3. **Click** on **Edit** in the menu bar. A pull-down menu sill appear.

4. **Click** on **Duplicate**. A duplicate slide will appear as slide 5.

5. **Click twice** on the new **slide 5** to move to Slide view.

Notice that PowerPoint duplicated the slide exactly, including the rectangle and the 75% zoom view.

GROUPING ELEMENTS

In this section, you will combine the rectangle and #1 into a single element so that they always stay together. First, you will use the mouse arrow to "lasso" them together.

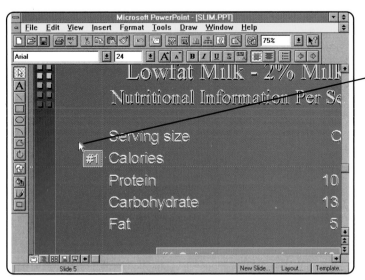

1. **Place** the mouse arrow **above and** to the **left** of the **rectangle**, as you see in this example.

2. **Press and hold** the mouse button and **drag** the cursor **down and** to the **right**. As you drag, you will see a dotted rectangle form a lasso around the rectangle and text block.

3. **Release** the mouse button when you have *completely* enclosed the elements within the lasso. The lasso will disappear.

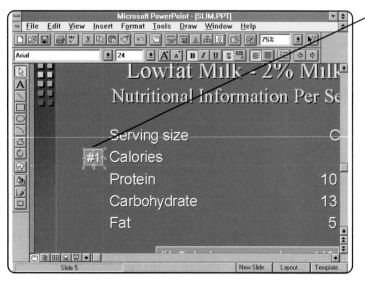

Notice that the lassoed block now has double handles. The *double handles* show that you have selected two elements.

4. Click on **Draw** in the menu bar. A pull-down menu will appear.

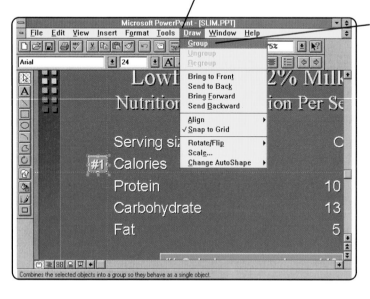

5. Click on **Group**. The pull-down menu will disappear. The two blocks are now grouped. *Grouped* means that the two blocks will be treated as a single unit when you move or edit them. In the next section, you will move the grouped block.

MOVING A GROUPED ELEMENT

1. **Move** the **horizontal guide** so that it is **below** the word **"Fat."**

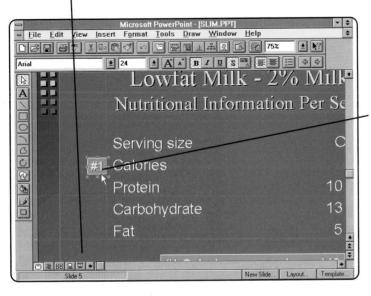

2. **Press and hold** the **Shift key** and **click** on the **#1 square** if it doesn't already have selection handles.

3. **Place** the arrow on the **border**, but be careful not to place it on a handle.

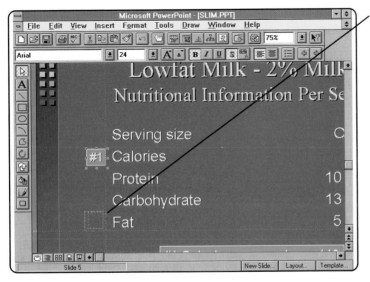

4. **Press and hold** the mouse button and **drag** the **dotted square** to the **intersection** of the **guides** you placed by "Fat."

5. **Release** the mouse button. The #1 block will snap to the guides next to the word "Fat."

EDITING TEXT IN A GROUPED ELEMENT

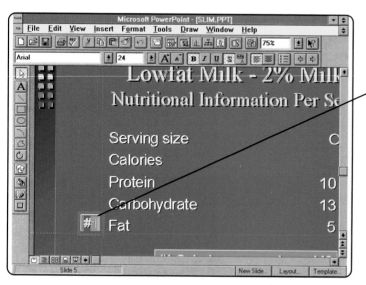

This process is exactly the same as editing text that isn't grouped.

1. **Drag** the I-beam **over** the "1" but not over the # sign.

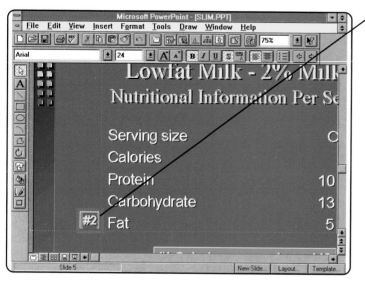

2. **Type 2**.

3. **Click anywhere off** the **text block to** deselect it.

Changing the View

1. **Click once** in the **Zoom Control box** to **highlight 75%**.

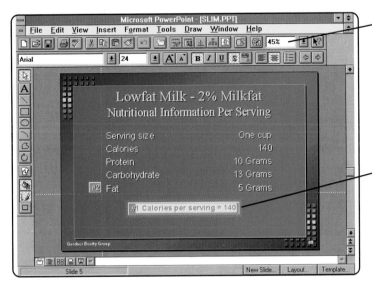

2. **Type 45** and **press Enter.** Your view will change back to 45%.

Adding Text to a Text Block

1. **Drag** the I-beam cursor **over 1 Calories per serving = 140** to select it. You don't have to highlight the # sign because you're not going to change it.

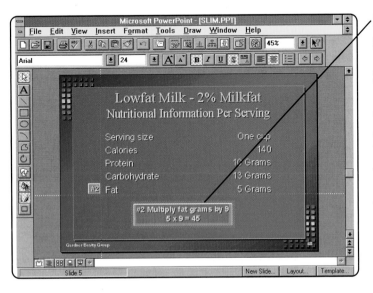

2. **Type 2 Multiply fat grams by 9.**

3. **Press Enter.**

4. **Type 5 x 9 = 45.** It will be centered on the next line because you centered the text in this block in "Centering text and a text block" in Chapter 6.

USING RULERS

In this section, you will use the rulers as guides for changing the size of the text block.

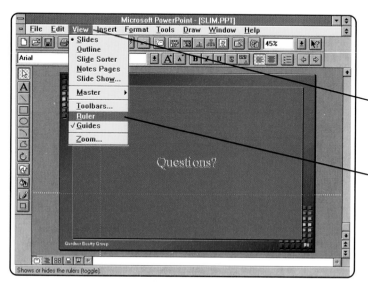

1. Press the **Page Down key** on your keyboard **twice** to move to **slide 7**.

2. Click on **View** in the menu bar. A pull-down menu will appear.

3. Click on **Ruler**. Rulers will appear at the top and left of the slide.

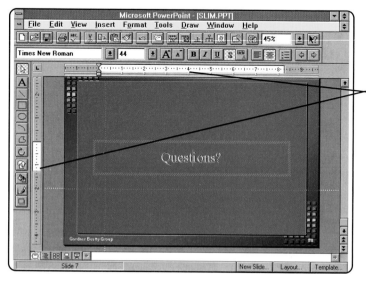

4. Click on **Questions?** to select it. The text block will be surrounded by a border.

Notice that the rulers change size to show the size of the selected text box.

5. Click off the **text block** to deselect it.

6. **Move** your mouse pointer **around** the **slide**. Notice that the pointer's exact location is shown by dotted lines in the rulers. As you move the mouse pointer, the dotted lines move.

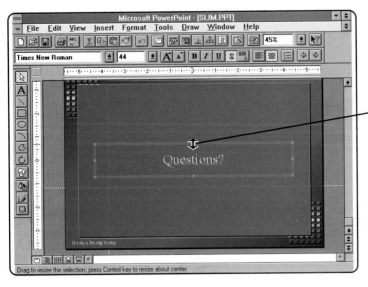

7. **Press and hold** the **Shift key** and **click** on the **text** to select the text block with handles.

8. **Place** the cursor on the **top middle handle**. The cursor becomes a double-headed arrow.

9. **Press and hold** the mouse button. The double-headed arrow will become a plus sign.

10. **Continue** to **hold** the mouse button as you **drag** the cursor **up** until it **reaches** the **1.5"** mark on the vertical ruler.

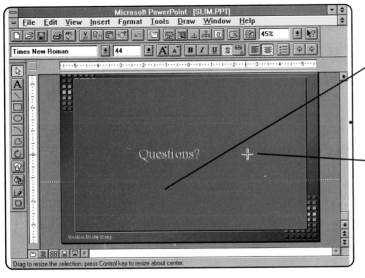

11. **Release** the mouse button.

12. **Repeat steps 8 through 11** to **move** the **bottom edge** of the **text block down** to **1.5."**

13. **Repeat steps 8 through 11**, using the horizontal ruler to **decrease** the **width** of the **text box to 2.5"** on each side.

USING CHANGE AutoShape

In this section, you will change the shape of the text block. Then you will fill in the text block with color and add a line around the border.

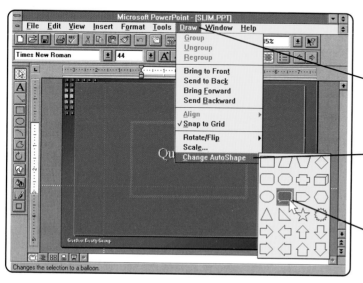

1. **Click** on the **text block** if it is not already selected.

2. **Click** on **Draw** in the menu bar. A pull-down menu will appear.

3. **Click** on **Change AutoShape**. An AutoShape box will appear.

4. **Click** on the **text balloon shape** in the third row.

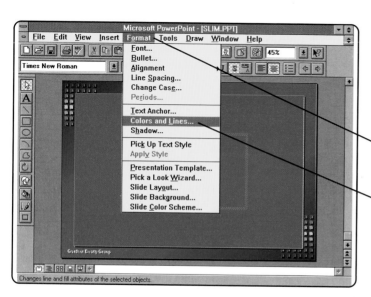

Notice that nothing seems to have changed. The new shape really is there; you just need to format it with the fill and line color.

5. **Click** on **Format** in the menu bar.

6. **Click** on **Colors and Lines**. A colors and Lines dialog box will appear.

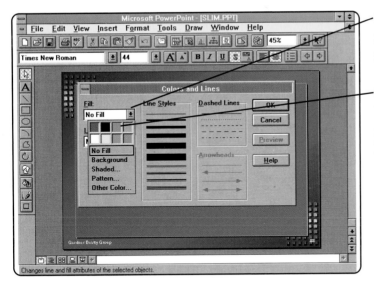

7. **Click** on the ⬇ to the **right** of **No Fill**. A color menu will appear.

8. **Click** on the **dark pink box**. (For color-blind folks, it's the third box from the left in the top row.)

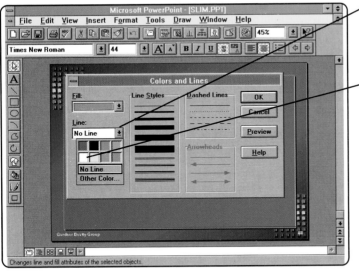

9. **Click** on the ⬇ to the **right** of **No Line**. A color menu will appear.

10. **Click** on the **white block**. The line box will become white.

11. **Click** on **OK**. The text block will appear with the new shape and colors.

ADDING A SHADOW TO A TEXT BLOCK

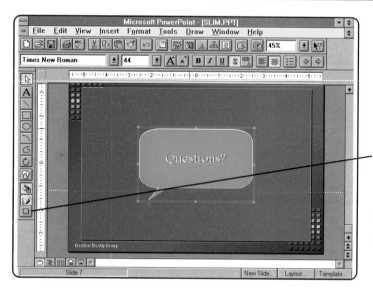

It is very easy to enhance a shape by adding a shadow to it.

1. **Click** on the **text block** if it isn't already selected.

2. **Click** on the **Shadow tool** in the drawing toolbar.

Notice the shadow on the right and bottom of the text box.

Turning Off Rulers and Guides

1. **Click** on **View** in the menu bar.

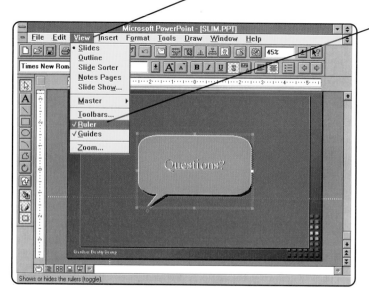

2. **Click** on **Ruler** to *remove* the checkmark and turn off the rulers.

3. **Repeat steps 1 and 2**, clicking on Guides instead of Rulers, to remove the guides.

CREATING AN AutoShape

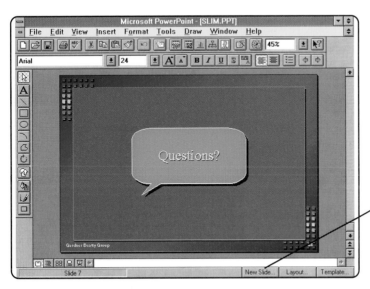

Now it's time to play! In this section, you will create a new slide so that you can play with making and changing AutoShapes. If you are following along with this presentation, you will not save this new slide to the slim.ppt file.

1. **Click** on **New Slide**. The New Slide dialog box will appear.

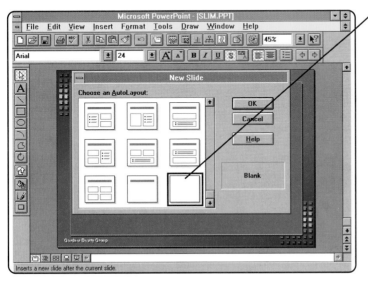

2. **Click twice** on the **Blank slide** at the **bottom** of the **Auto Layout text box**. A blank slide will appear.

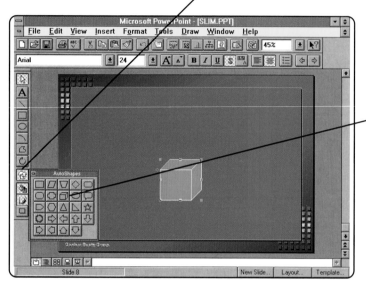

3. **Click** on the **AutoShapes tool**, which is the fourth from the bottom on the Drawing toolbar. A pop-up box of shapes will appear. It may be a different size than you see in this example.

4. **Click** on **any shape you want**. In this example, we chose the Cube tool.

5. **Place** the mouse pointer on the slide. Notice that the pointer turns into a cross.

6. **Press and hold** the mouse button and **drag** it **over** the slide to draw the cube. Notice that as long as you hold the mouse button, you can drag up, down, and sideways to change the shape and orientation of the object.

7. **Release** the mouse button when the cube is in the shape you want.

Changing AutoShapes

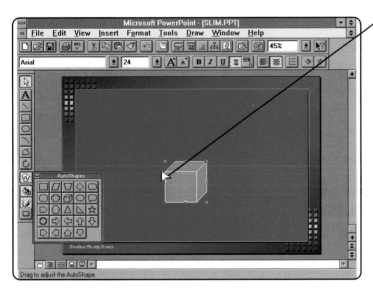

1. **Place** the mouse pointer on the **small diamond-shaped handle**. The mouse pointer will change into an arrowhead.

2. **Press and hold** the mouse button as you **drag** it to the **right** to change the dimension of the cube. Notice how easily you can change the shape of the object by moving the cursor back and forth. Notice also that you can change the shape of the object only within the parameters of the original shape. You cannot use the diamond to make the new shape bigger than the original. Use the handles to change the size of an object.

3. **Release** the mouse button when you find the right shape.

Deleting a Slide

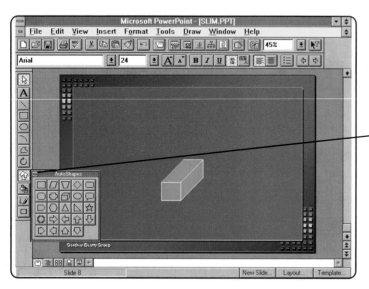

Because this slide was created just so you could practice drawing shapes, you can delete it from the presentation.

1. Click on the **Control menu button** on the AutoShapes menu bar. The box will disappear.

2. Click on **Edit** in the menu bar.

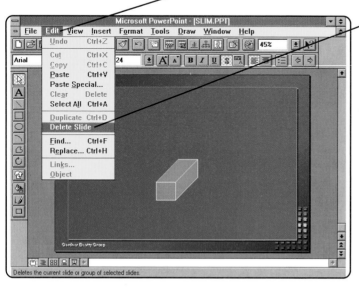

3. Click on **Delete Slide**. The newly created slide 8 will disappear, and slide 7 will appear on your screen.

Remember to save your work if you are continuing on to the next chapter.

Working with Clip Art

Pictures can do wonderful things for your presentation. PowerPoint has more than 1,100 color clip-art images specially designed for use in a presentation. In this chapter you will do the following:

❖ Learn two ways to add clip art to slides

❖ Move, size, and color clip art

❖ Rotate an object

CHANGING SLIDE LAYOUT

In this section, you will change the layout of a slide and then add clip art to the slide.

1. **Press and hold** the mouse button and **drag** the scroll button toward the **top** of the **scroll bar**.

2. **Release** the mouse button when slide 3 appears to the left of the scroll bar. Slide 3 will appear on your screen.

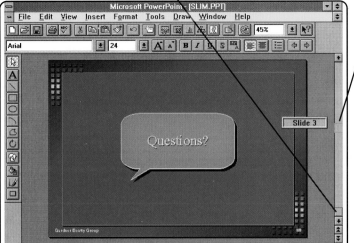

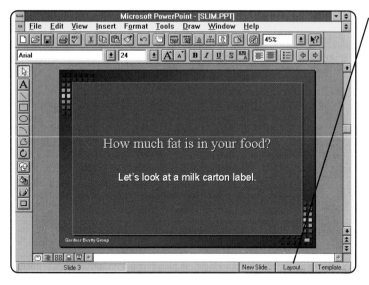

3. Click on **Layout**. The Slide Layout dialog box will appear.

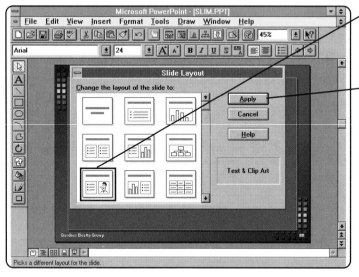

4. Click on the **Text and Clip Art slide** in the first column on the third row.

5. Click on **Apply**. The layout of slide 3 will be changed.

ADDING CLIP ART

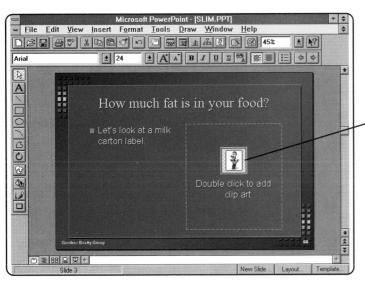

If you are opening up the clip-art library for the first time, PowerPoint will have to load the files. Be patient; this will take a few minutes.

1. Click twice on the **Clip Art Gallery button**. If your clip art has already been loaded, you will see the screen at the top of the next page. If this is the first time you are using the clip-art library, Power-Point will ask if you want to add clip art.

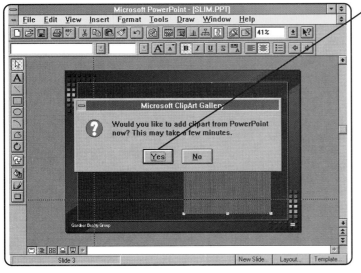

2. Click on **Yes**. A Microsoft message will appear that says, "Please wait...The ClipArt Gallery is adding pictures. If you should change your mind, click on Cancel.

Notice there are 26 categories of clip art from which to choose.

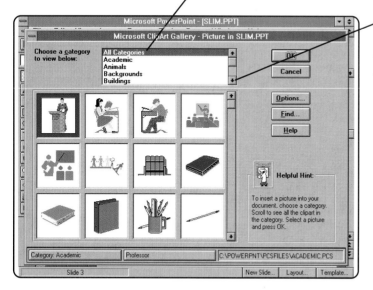

In each category, you can view the selection of clip art by using the scroll bar button to the right of the clip art.

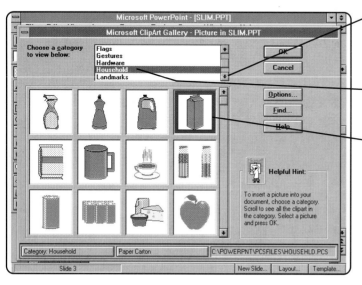

3. Click repeatedly on the ↓ on the scroll bar to **scroll down** the list to **Household**.

4. Click on **Household** to highlight it.

5. Click on the **milk carton**, which is the last picture on the top row. It will be surrounded by a thick selection border.

6. Click on **OK**. The clip art will appear on slide 3.

SIZING CLIP ART

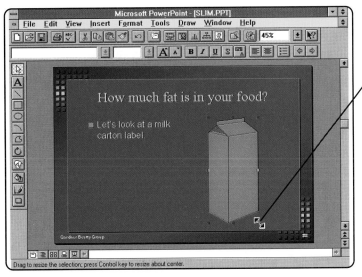

In this section, you will fine-tune the clip art by changing its size.

1. Click on **the clip art** if it is not already selected. Solid squares, or handles, will appear on the border of the clip art.

2. Place the mouse arrow on the **bottom right handle**. The mouse pointer will become a two-headed arrow.

3. Press and hold the mouse button. The two-headed arrow will change into a plus sign, and a dotted rectangle will appear around the milk carton. **Drag** the plus sign **diagonally up** and to the **left** to size the carton proportionally.

4. Release the mouse button when you have the desired size. You may have to fiddle with steps 1 through 3 until the milk carton is sized the way you want it.

MOVING CLIP ART

There are two ways to move clip art.

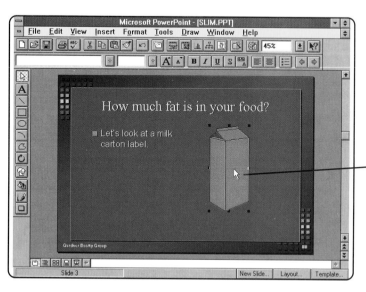

Dragging Clip Art

1. **Click** anywhere on the **milk carton** if it isn't already selected.

2. **Press and hold** the mouse button and **drag** the cursor to **reposition** the **milk carton** to the **right**.

3. **Release** the mouse button.

Moving Clip Art with the Arrow Key

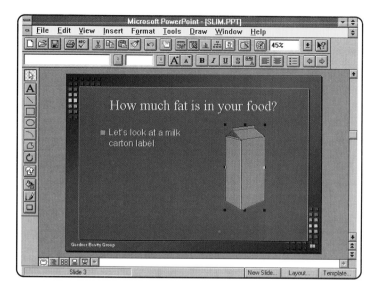

You can fine-tune the placement of graphics (and text blocks) by using the arrow keys to "nudge" the graphic in a specific direction.

1. **Click** on the **milk carton** if it does not already have selection handles.

2. **Press** the → **key** on your keyboard. The graphic will move slightly to the right. Experiment with the other arrow keys.

RECOLORING CLIP ART

In this section, you will change the red color in the clip art to another color.

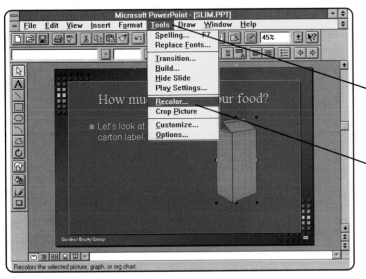

1. **Click** on the **clip art** if it doesn't already have selection handles.

2. **Click** on **Tools** in the menu bar. A pull-down menu will appear.

3. **Click** on **Recolor**. The Recolor Picture dialog box will appear.

4. **Click** on the ⬇ **beside** the **red color block**. A drop-down list will appear.

5. **Click** on **Other Color**. The Other Color dialog box will appear.

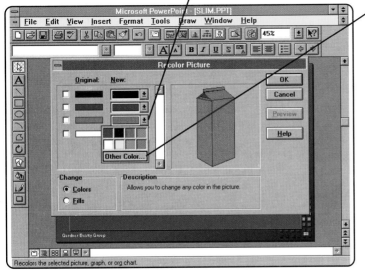

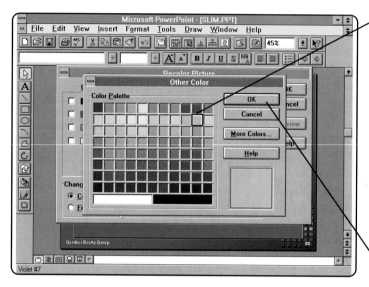

6. Click on the **purple square**, which is the second square from the end on the second row.

Notice that a preview of the color will appear in the preview box and the name of the color will appear at the bottom of your screen. In this example, the color is Violet #7.

7. Click on **OK**. The Recolor Picture dialog box will appear.

8. Click on **Preview** to see how the object will look with the new color.

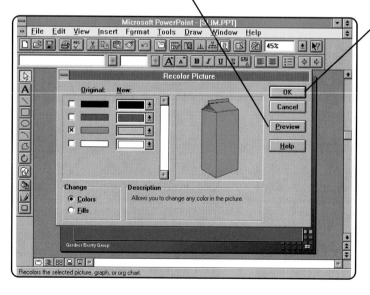

9. Click on **OK**. Slide 3 will reappear with the new color on the milk carton.

ADDING CLIP ART WITH THE INSERT MENU

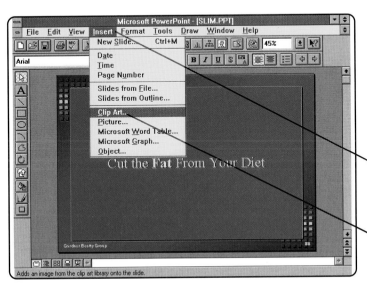

In this section, you will add clip art to a slide by using the Insert menu.

1. Press the **Page Up key two times** to change the view to slide 1.

2. Click on **Insert** in the menu bar. A drop-down list will appear.

3. Click on **Clip Art**. The Microsoft ClipArt Gallery will appear.

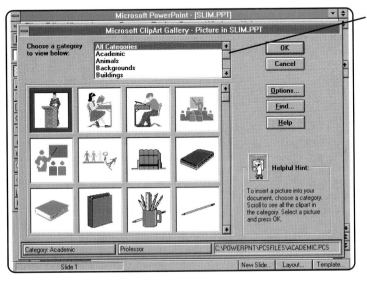

4. Move the mouse arrow to the **scroll button** in the **Categories** list.

5. Press and hold the mouse button and **drag** the scroll button **down** the scroll bar to the **Household** category.

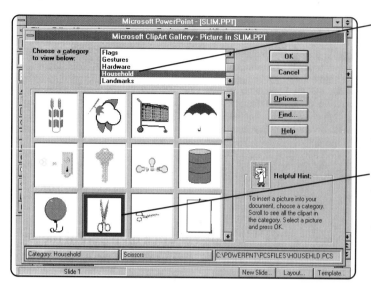

6. **Click** on the **Household** category to highlight it.

7. **Click four times** on the ⬇ on the scroll bar until the picture of the scissors appears.

8. **Click** on the **scissors** in the second row.

9. **Click** on **OK**.

CHANGING CLIP-ART WIDTH

You can change just the width of clip art by using the center handle on the left or right of the clip art.

1. **Click** on **the clip-art image** if it isn't already selected. Solid squares, or *handles*, will appear on the border of the clip art.

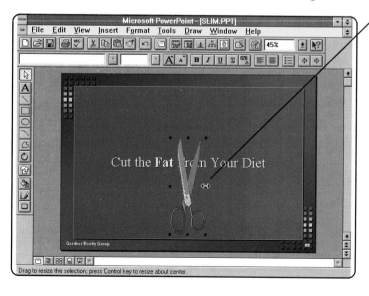

2. **Place** the mouse pointer on the **center handle** on the **right side** of the **scissors**. The pointer will become a two-headed arrow.

3. **Press and hold** the mouse button. It will become a plus sign, and a dotted rectangle will appear around the scissors.

4. **Drag** the handle to the **right** to widen the scissors and then **release** the mouse button.

Undoing a Change

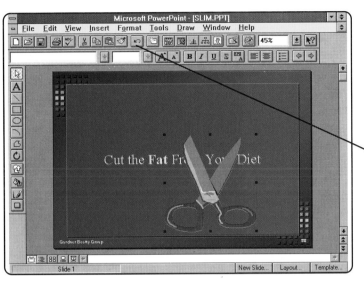

In this example, you don't want the scissors to be extra wide. You can use the Undo feature to undo or reverse a change if you use it before you do any other function.

1. **Click** on the **Undo button** in the toolbar. The picture will be returned to the size it was before you widened it.

Changing the Overall Size of Clip Art

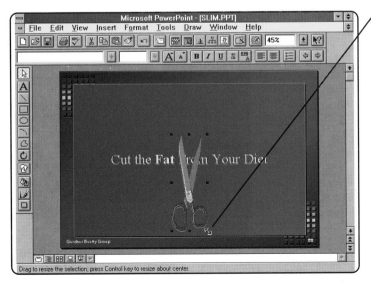

1. **Place** the mouse arrow on the bottom right handle. It will turn into a two-headed arrow.

2. **Press and hold** the mouse button as you **drag** the arrow **diagonally up and** to the **left** to reduce the size of the scissors proportionally.

3. **Release** the mouse button when you have the desired size. You may have to repeat steps 1 and 2 until the scissors are sized as you see on the next page.

ROTATING AN OBJECT

Before you rotate the scissors, you'll move them to the top half of the slide and convert them to a PowerPoint object.

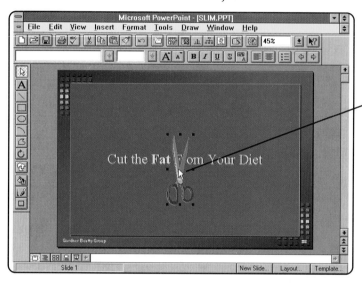

Moving Clip Art

1. Place the mouse arrow on the **scissors**.

2. Press and hold the mouse button and **drag** the cursor to move the scissors **above** the word "the" as in the next example. Then **release** the mouse button.

Converting Clip Art to a PowerPoint Object

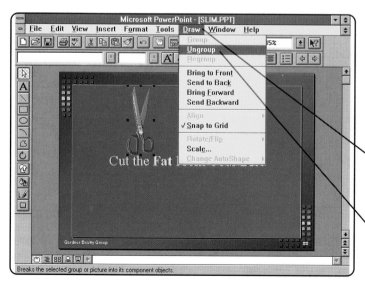

Normally, only objects that are drawn in PowerPoint can be rotated. To rotate clip art, it is necessary to complete the following steps:

1. Click on **Draw** in the menu bar. A pull-down menu will appear.

2. Click on **Ungroup**. A Microsoft PowerPoint message box will appear.

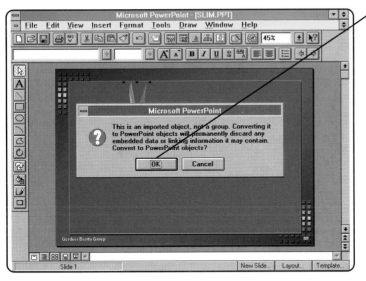

3. Click on **OK**. The scissors with lots of selection handles will appear in the window. In the next step, you will group the scissors as a PowerPoint object.

4. Click on **Draw** in the menu bar. A pull-down menu will appear.

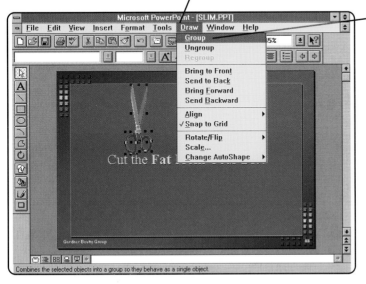

5. Click on **Group**. The scissors are now considered a PowerPoint object and can be rotated.

Applying the Rotation

In this section, you will change the orientation of the clip art.

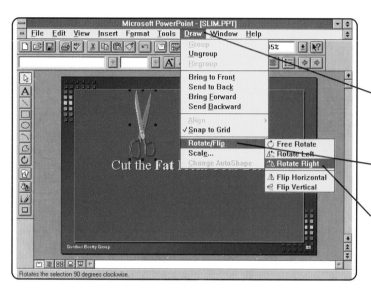

1. **Click** on the **scissors** if they are not already selected.

2. **Click** on **Draw** in the menu bar. A pull-down menu will appear.

3. **Click** on **Rotate/Flip**. A second menu will appear.

4. **Click** on **Rotate Right**.

Notice that the scissors have rotated 90 degrees to the right.

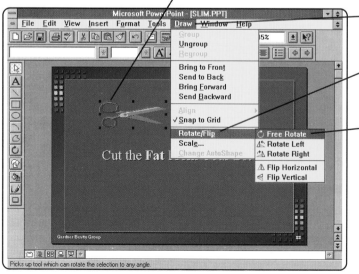

5. **Click** on **Draw**. A pull-down menu will appear.

6. **Click** on **Rotate/Flip**. A second menu will appear.

7. **Click** on **Free Rotate**. The mouse arrow will turn into a circular design.

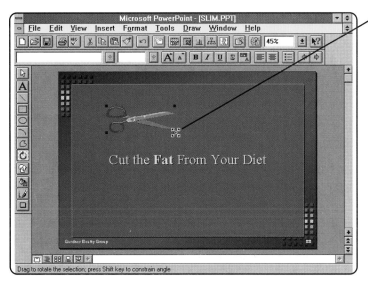

8. **Click** and **hold** the **lower-right section handle**. The cursor will change to the shape you see in this example.

9. **Drag** the **selection handle** toward "Fat." An outline of the scissors will rotate as you drag.

10. **Release** the mouse button when the scissors point toward "Fat."

11. **Click** on the **background** to release the rotation tool.

12. **C**lick on the **scissors** and **use** the mouse pointer to move the scissors to the position you see in the next example.

Adding a Shadow to Clip Art

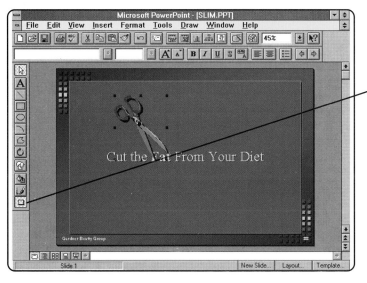

1. **Click** on the **scissors** if they are not already selected.

2. **Click** on the **Shadow button** in the Drawing toolbar. A shadow will be added.

Sending an Object to the Back

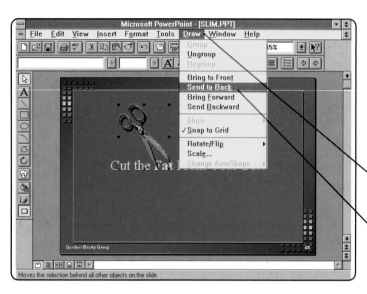

It is necessary to send the object to the back of the slide so that the scissors will not print on top of the text.

1. **Click** on the **scissors** if they are not already selected.

2. **Click** on **Draw**. A pull-down menu will appear.

3. **Click** on **Send to Back**.

4. **Click anywhere** on the **slide** to deselect the object.

Saving the Slide

1. **Click** on the **Save button** in the toolbar. The clip art that has been added to your slides will now be saved to the slim.ppt file.

You'll do some fun things with WordArt in the next chapter.

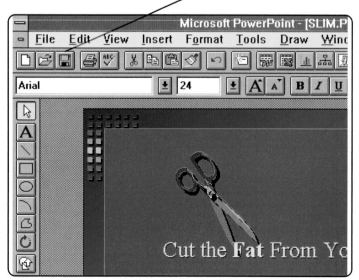

Creating Special Effects with WordArt

Sometimes a slide just needs that little extra pizzazz. PowerPoint 4.0 allows you to access two special sub-programs, WordArt 1 and WordArt 2, to help you embellish your presentations. However, WordArt 1 is available *only* if you have previously installed Microsoft Word 2 or Microsoft Publisher. WordArt 2 comes with only PowerPoint 4.0 and a few other Microsoft programs.

The significant difference between the two programs is that WordArt 1 contains 19 special fonts that are included with it, and WordArt 2 uses only the TrueType fonts you have loaded on your system. In this chapter you will do the following:

❖ Create a special effect using WordArt 1
❖ Create a special effect using WordArt 2

USING WORDART 1

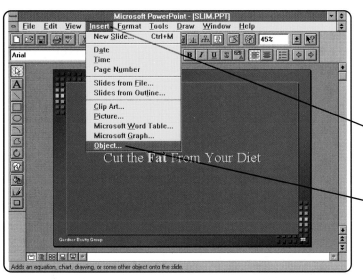

In this section, you will embellish the title on slide 1.

1. **Open slim.ppt** to slide 1 if it isn't already open.

2. **Click** on **Insert** in the menu bar. A pull-down menu will appear.

3. **Click** on **Objec**t. The Insert Object dialog box will appear.

4. **Click repeatedly** on the ⬇ to scroll through the programs available on your system.

5. **Click** on **Microsoft WordArt 1.0 or MS WordArt** to select it. If you don't see WordArt 1 or MS WordArt, it means that you don't have it available on your system. (WordArt does not come with PowerPoint 4, but it did come with Word 2 and some other programs.) So, simply go on to step 4 in the "Using WordArt 2" section later in this chapter.

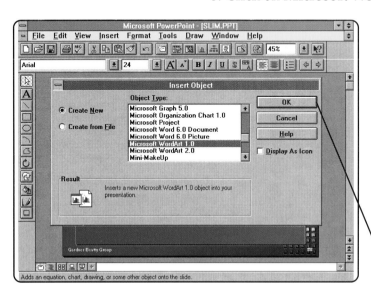

6. **Click** on **OK**. A Microsoft WordArt dialog box will appear.

Notice that "Your Text Here" is already highlighted and can be seen in the Preview box, showing the font, size, style, fill, and alignment that are listed in the boxes to the left.

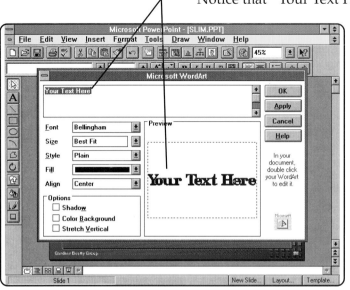

ENTERING AND STYLING TEXT IN WORDART 1

1. **Type fat**.

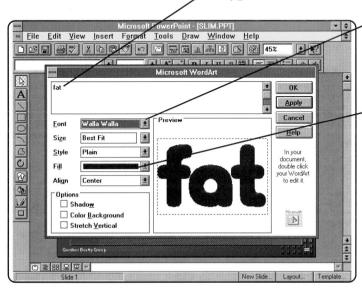

2. **Click** on the ⬇ to the **right** of the **Font box**. A pull-down menu will appear.

3. **Click repeatedly** on the ⬇ to **scroll down** to the **end** of the **list** and **click** on **Walla Walla**.

Notice that the word "fat" has changed from Bellingham to the Walla Walla font in the Preview box.

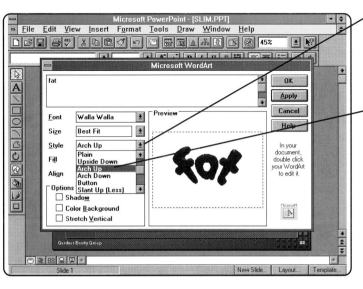

4. **Click** on the ⬇ to the **right** of the **Style box**. A pull-down menu will appear.

5. **Click** on **Arch Up**.

Notice that the new style is shown in the Preview box.

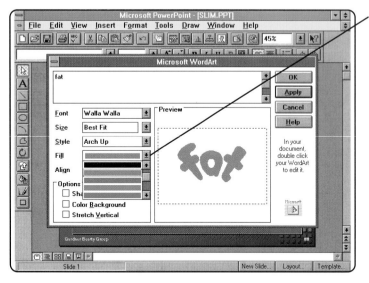

6. Click on the ⬇ to the **right** of the **fill box**. A pull-down menu of colored bars will appear.

7. Click on the **red bar** to select it.

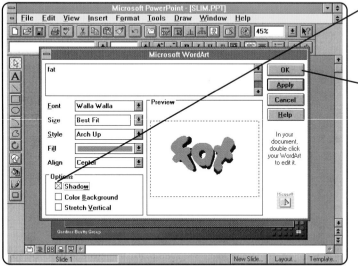

8. Click on **Shadow** in the Options box to place an ✕ to the left of Shadow.

9. Click on **OK**. The WordArt dialog box will disappear.

COMBINING WORDART WITH A TEXT LINE

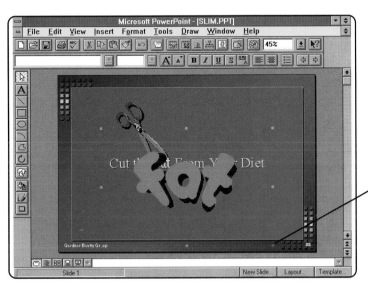

Because WordArt is created as an object, PowerPoint won't allow you to combine it with regular text in a text line. But, with a slightly fussy "work-around," you can make it look as though it all fits together.

1. **Click on and hold** the **bottom right corner handle** of the WordArt and **drag up and** to the **left** to **resize** it smaller. This is only to get it out of the way for now, so the exact size doesn't matter. If you need help with this, refer to Chapter 11, "Working with Clip Art."

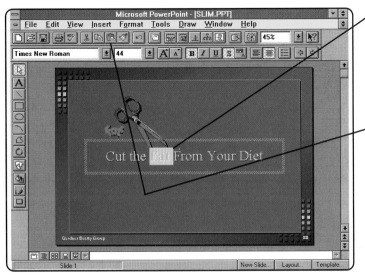

2. **Click and hold** just after the **t** in **Fat** *in the text block.*

3. **Drag** the cursor to the **left** to **highlight** the word **Fat**.

4. **Click** on the **Cut button** in the toolbar. "Fat" will disappear. (We should all be so lucky.)

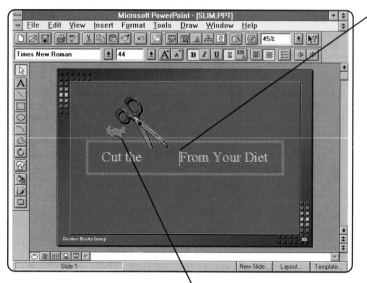

5. Press the **spacebar repeatedly** until you make room for the WordArt.

6. Click on the **"fat" WordArt** to get the selection handles.

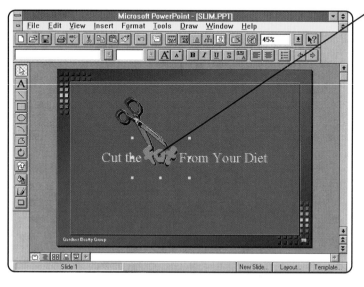

7. Press and hold the mouse button and **drag** the **WordArt** into the **space between** "the" and "From."

8. Click on, **hold**, **and drag** a **corner handle** to **resize** the **WordArt** to fit the space, as you see in this example. If you need help with this, refer to Chapter 11, "Working with Clip Art." Remember that you can use the arrow keys to make fine adjustments in the position of the Word Art.

Grouping WordArt and Text

1. Click on the **WordArt** if it doesn't already have selection handles.

2. Press and hold the **Shift key** and **click** on the **text block** to select both at the same time.

3. Release the **Shift key**.

4. Click on **Draw** in the menu bar. A pull-down menu will appear.

5. Click on **Group**.

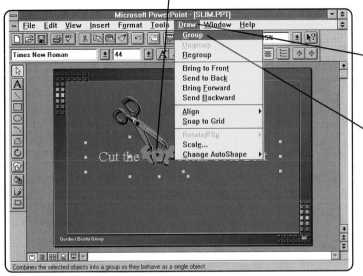

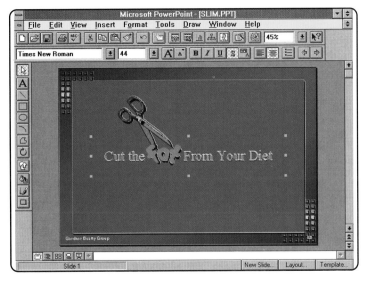

The text line and the WordArt can now be moved as a single element!

USING WORDART 2

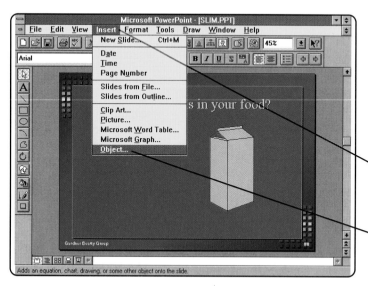

In this section, you will create a label for the milk carton on slide 3.

1. Press the **Page Down key twice** to move to slide 3 in slim.ppt.

2. Click on **Insert** in the menu bar. A pull-down menu will appear.

3. Click on **Object**. The Insert Object dialog box will appear.

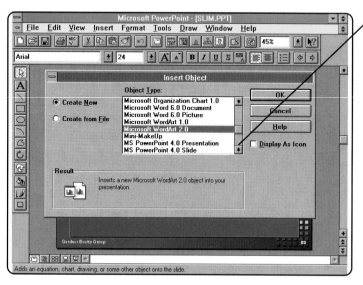

4. Click repeatedly on the ↓ to scroll through the available programs.

5. Click on **Microsoft WordArt 2.0** to select it.

6. Click on **OK**.

Notice that the menu bar now shows the WordArt command buttons.

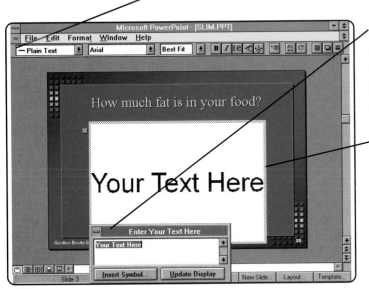

The text entry box can be moved by placing the arrow on the title bar. Then press, hold, and drag to a more convenient position.

The preview box shows how your text will look.

ENTERING TEXT IN WORDART 2

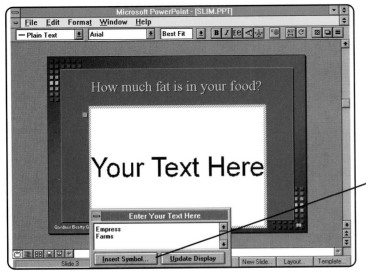

1. **Type Empress**. It will replace the highlighted text. **Press Enter**.

2. **Type Farms**.

Inserting a Symbol

1. With the cursor placed just after "Farms," **click** on **Insert Symbol**. An Insert Symbol dialog box will appear.

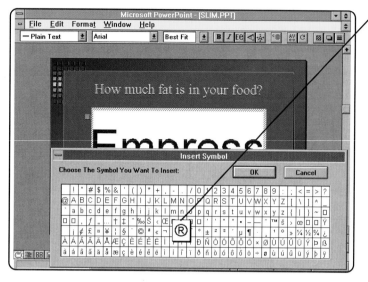

2. Click on the ® in the middle of the fifth row.

3. Click on **OK**. The Insert Symbol dialog box will disappear.

4. Click just **after** the ®. **Press Enter**.

5. Type LowFat. Press Enter.

6. Type Milk.

FORMATTING TEXT IN WORDART 2

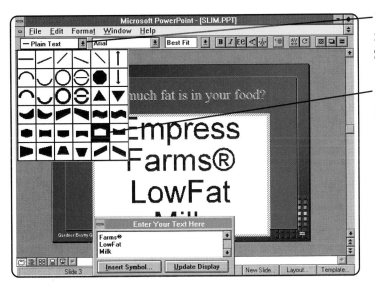

1. **Click** on the ⬇ to the **right** of the **shape box**. A Shape menu will appear.

2. **Click** on the **Inflate Top Shape button**.

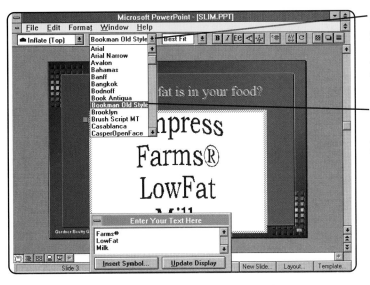

3. **Click** on the ⬇ to the **right** of the **Font box**. A pull-down menu will appear.

4. **Click** on **Bookman Old Style** or whichever font you like if you don't have this one.

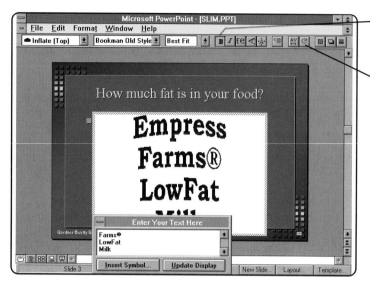

5. Click on the **Bold button (B)**.

6. Click on the **Rotate button**, which is the fourth button from the right. A Special Effects dialog box will appear.

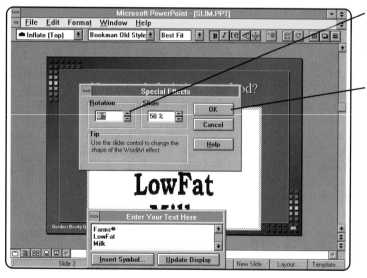

7. Click on the ▲ to the **right of 0*** to change it to **10***.

8. Click on **OK**.

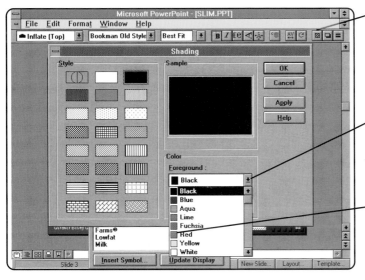

9. **Click** on the **Shading button**, which is the third button from the right. A Shading dialog box will appear.

10. **Click** on ⬇ below Foreground in the Color box. A color menu will appear.

11. **Click** on **Red** to select it. The boxes to the left will turn red.

12. **Click** on **OK**.

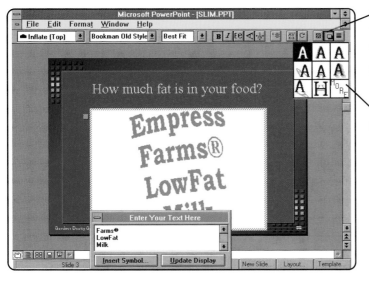

13. **Click** on the **Shadow button**, which is the second button from the right. A Shadow menu will appear.

14. **Click** on **More** to see the Shadow dialog box.

15. Click on the **second shadow** box to select it.

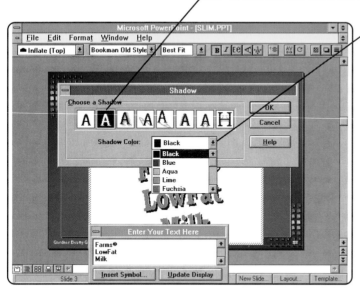

16. Click on the ⬇ to the **right** of **Shadow Color**. A color menu will appear.

17. Scroll to the **top** of the list and **click** on **black**.

18. Click on **OK**. The Shadow dialog box will disappear.

19. Click on the **slide background**. The WordArt text entry and preview boxes will disappear. The WordArt object will be placed in the middle of your slide, ready to be sized and placed into position.

If you're using a WordArt picture as an independent graphic, treat it just like a piece of clip art or other object. Placement, moving, and sizing are done as shown in Chapter 11, "Working with Clip Art."

20. Click twice on the **WordArt** to edit it. This will bring up the Enter Your Text Here dialog box.

Fiddle to your heart's content with the rotation angle, sizing, colors, etc.

Program Manager

Part III: Graphs, Tables, and Charts

Working with Graphs

To create a graph, you must first create a *datasheet*, or spreadsheet. You can create the datasheet in PowerPoint using a predesigned graph slide. If you already have a spreadsheet and graph in Excel, you can insert them into PowerPoint. You can also use a special toolbar button to take you into Excel. In this chapter you will do the following:

❖ Create a graph in PowerPoint
❖ Open a new presentation file
❖ Insert a graph from Excel into PowerPoint
❖ Use the Insert Microsoft Excel Worksheet button

CREATING A
GRAPH IN POWERPOINT

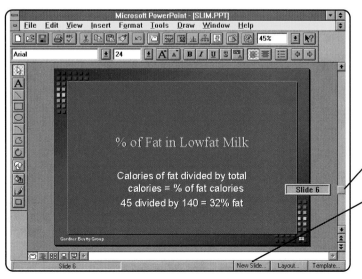

To create a graph, you must first create a datasheet. PowerPoint has a predesigned slide that makes this task really easy. In this section, you will add the graph slide after slide 6.

1. **Go to slide 6**.

2. **Click** on **New Slide**. The New Slide dialog box will appear.

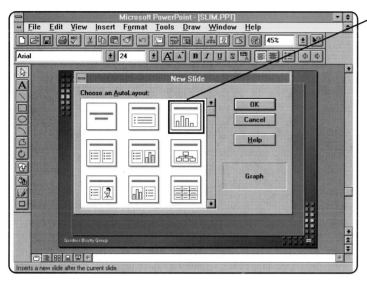

3. **Click** twice on the **Graph slide**, which is the last slide in the top row. The graph slide will appear in slide view.

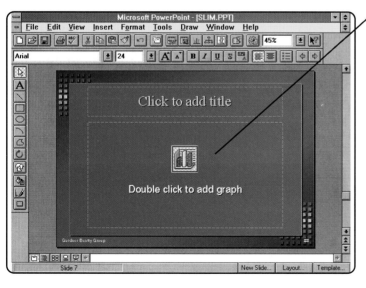

4. **Click twice inside** the **graph block**. You will see an hourglass, and your computer will make "computer-at-work" crunching noises as it brings up the PowerPoint datasheet, or spreadsheet.

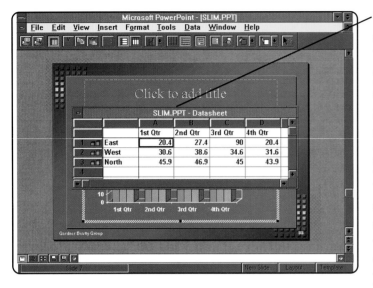

This is the datasheet that comes with PowerPoint. You can modify it just as you would any other spreadsheet. If you are familiar with Excel (or another spreadsheet program), you probably know everything you need to modify the existing datasheet. Giving step-by-step directions on working with spreadsheets is beyond the scope of this book, however. If you need help, refer to *Excel 5 for Windows*, another book in the *Visual Learning Guide* series.

This section will use a datasheet that has been modified, as you see here. Notice that we deleted the data in column D, increased the width of columns A and B, and changed the actual data. If you want to go through the steps in this process without changing the data, simply use the existing datasheet.

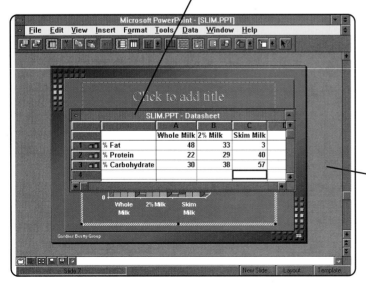

5. **Click anywhere** on the background. PowerPoint will automatically convert the datasheet into a graph and insert the graph into the slide. It couldn't be easier!

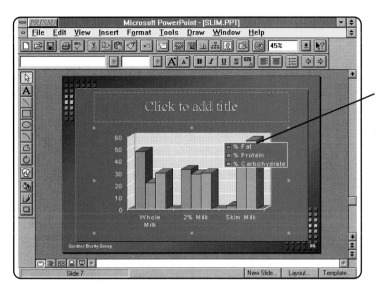

MOVING THE LEGEND

If the legend is on top of your graph, complete the following steps to move it.

1. Click twice on the **graph**. It will be surrounded by a candy-striped border.

Notice that the toolbar has changed to an Excel toolbar.

2. Click on the **Legend button** in the toolbar. The legend will be removed from the graph.

3. Click once again on the Legend button. The legend will be restored to the graph but will be placed to the side of the graph.

5. Click on the **background** to insert the graph into the slide.

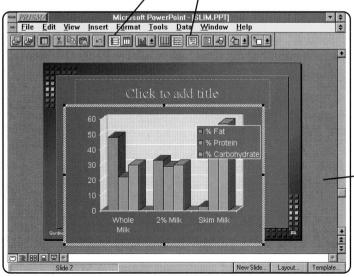

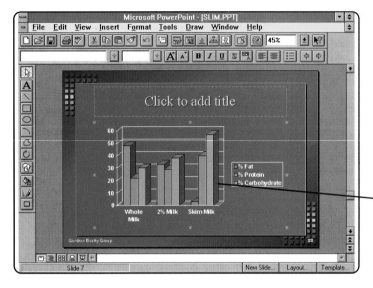

Isn't this terrific!

EDITING THE DATASHEET

You edit the contents of the graph by editing the datasheet.

1. **Click twice** on the **graph.** It will be surrounded by a candy-striped selection border. It is now the active element in the slide.

2. **Click** on **View** in the menu bar. A pull-down menu will appear.

3. **Click** on **Datasheet**. The datasheet will appear.

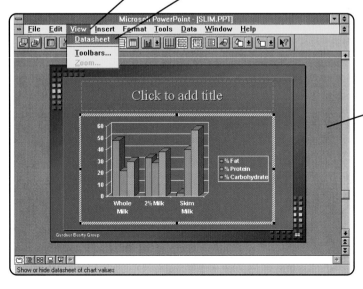

4. **Make** whatever **edits** you want. The changes will automatically be carried over to the graph.

5. **Click** on the **background** to insert the edited graph into the slide.

6. After the graph is inserted into the slide, **click** on the **background again** to remove the selection handles from the graph.

EDITING THE GRAPH

You can change the color and pattern of the bars. You can also change the grid behind the bars. These are just a few of the changes you can make in the graph.

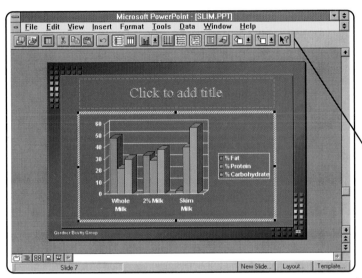

1. Click twice on the **graph**. It will be surrounded by a candy-striped selected border.

Notice that the buttons in the toolbar have changed to graph-related tools. Refer to *Excel 5 for Windows: The Visual Learning Guide* for details on how to change a graph.

Changing the Format of the Graph

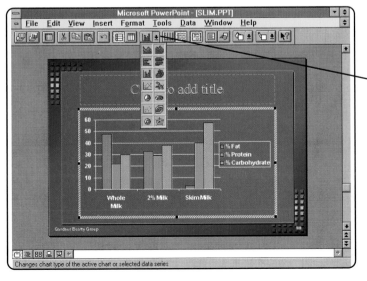

You can change the chart type with a click of your mouse.

1. While the graph is surrounded by the selection border, **click** on the ↓ to the **right of the Chart Type button** in the toolbar. A pull-down list of chart types will appear.

2. Click on the appropriate **chart type**. The graph will change to the selected type.

DELETING A TEXT BLOCK FROM A PREDESIGNED SLIDE

Normally, you would add a title to the graph that explains what the graph is about. However, if you've been following along with this book, you already know how to add a title, and the process wouldn't teach you anything new. So, for the purposes of this book, you will delete the title block that is part of this slide.

Just because a text block is on a predesigned slide doesn't mean that you have to use it. You can delete any text block you don't need.

1. **Click** on the **slide background** to deselect the chart.

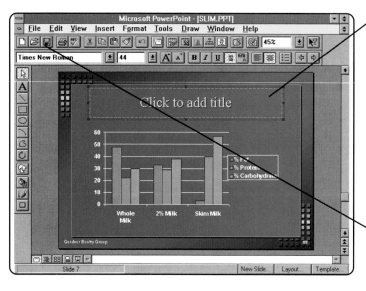

2. **Press and hold** the **Shift key** and **click inside** the **title text block**. This will select the block and at the same time add handles to the border.

3. **Press** the **Delete** (or Backspace) **key** to delete the text block from the slide.

4. **Click** on the **Save button** in the toolbar to save your work.

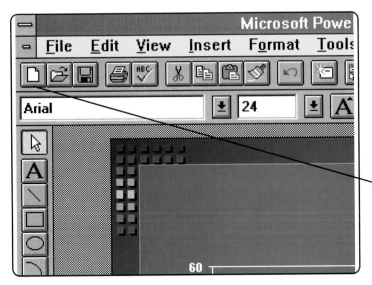

OPENING A NEW FILE

In this example, you will open a new file in preparation for the next section.

1. Click on the **New File button** in the toolbar. The New Presentation dialog box will appear.

2. Click on **Current Presentation Format** to put a dot in the circle. This will create a new presentation with the same template as the one you are currently using.

3. Click on **OK**. The Slide Layout dialog box will appear.

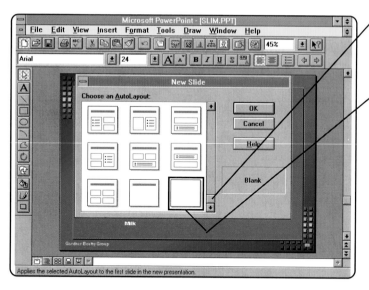

4. Press and hold the **scroll button** and **drag** it to the **bottom** of the **scroll bar**.

5. Click twice on the **Blank slide** in the last line. A blank slide will appear on your screen with the same formatting as the SLIM presentation.

IMPORTING AN EXISTING WORKSHEET

If you have a worksheet already created and saved in a spreadsheet program such as Excel or 1-2-3, you can import it into PowerPoint. In this section, you will import a worksheet from Excel.

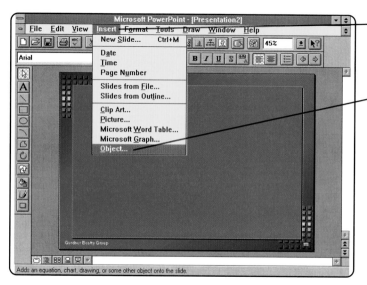

1. Click on **Insert** in the menu bar. A pull-down menu will appear.

2. Click on **Object**. The Insert Object dialog box will appear.

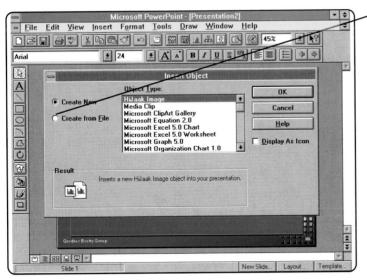

3. **Click** on **Create from File** to put a dot in the circle. The dialog box will change to show a Browse button.

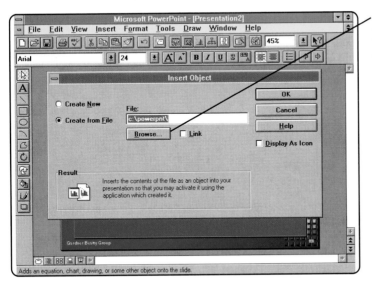

4. **Click** on **Browse**. The Browse dialog box will appear.

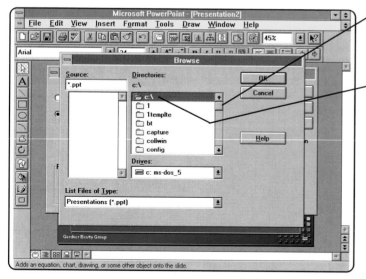

5. Drag the **scroll button** to the top of the scrollbar. You will see c:\.

6. Click twice on **c:**. A list of all the directories on your C drive will appear in the Directories list.

7. Scroll through the list of directories until you see the one that contains the file you want to import. In this example, the spreadsheet is contained in an "excelwrk" directory.

8. Click twice on the directory name.

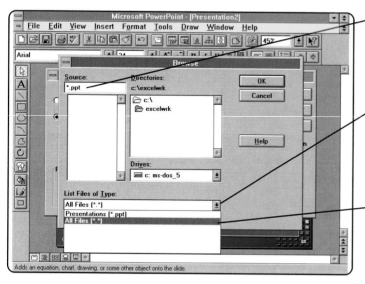

You'll notice that no files are listed in the Filename box. This is because the File type is still listed as ".ppt" files.

9. Click on the ⬇ to the right of the List Files of Type box. A pull-down list of file types will appear.

10. Click on **All Files [*.*]**. A list of all files in the directory will appear.

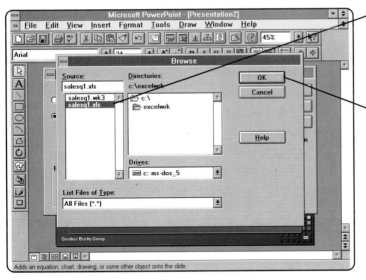

11. **Click** on the **name** of the file you want to import. In this example, it is salesq1.xls.

12. **Click** on **OK**. The Insert Object dialog box will appear.

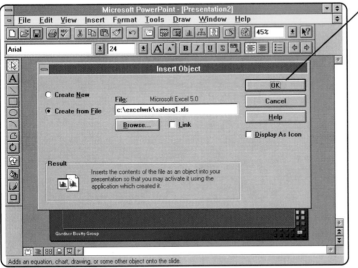

13. **Click** on **OK**. You will see an hourglass as PowerPoint imports the file. (The hourglass may last a while, so don't think you did anything wrong.)

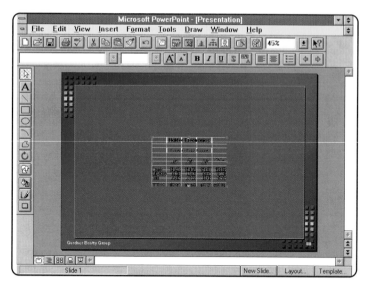

As you can see, the miniaturization gremlins have been at work and messed up the size of the worksheet. Fortunately, it's easy to fix.

SCALING AN OBJECT

You can, of course, drag a corner handle to enlarge the worksheet, but there is another way to accomplish the same thing.

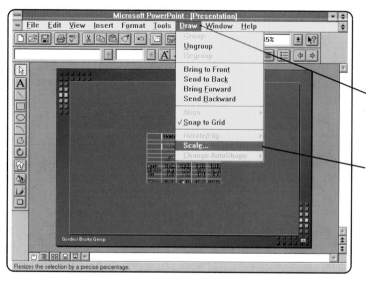

1. Click on the **worksheet** if it does not already have selection handles.

2. Click on **Draw** in the menu bar. A pull-down menu will appear.

3. Click on **Scale**. The Scale dialog box will appear.

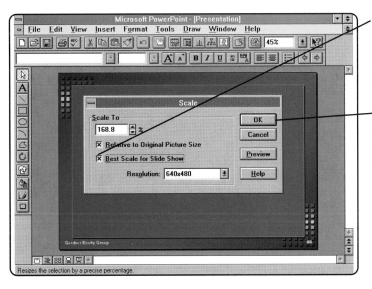

4. Click on **Best Scale for Slide Show** to put an ✕ in the box. Notice that the Scale To figure changes.

5. Click on **OK**. The worksheet will be resized proportionately.

EDITING A WORKSHEET

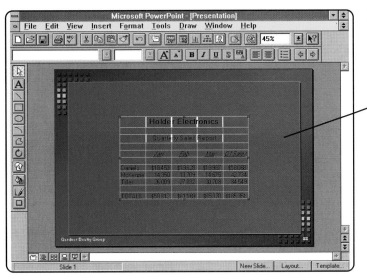

Notice that the gridlines are on the chart. If you don't want them, you can take them out in Excel.

1. Click twice on the **worksheet**. You will be taken into the original Excel file.

Removing Gridlines from an Imported Worksheet

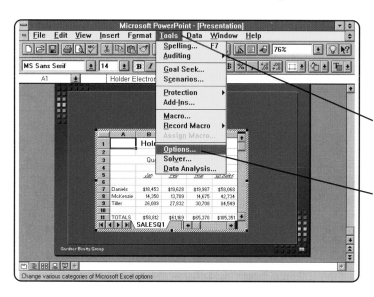

If you're using Excel 5, follow steps 1 through 5. If you're using Excel 4, see the note after step 5.

1. Click on **Tools** in the menu bar. A pull-down menu will appear.

2. Click on **Options** to see the Options dialog box.

3. Click on **View** if it is not already the front card in the dialog box.

4. Click on **Gridlines** to *remove* the X from the box.

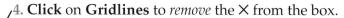

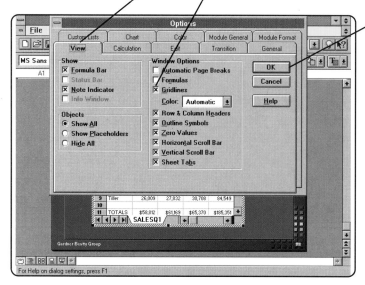

5. Click on **OK**. The gridlines will disappear.

(In Excel 4, row and column headings as well as gridlines will be copied with the graph. To delete them in Excel, click on Options in the menu bar, and then click on Display on the pull-down menu. In the Display dialog box, click on Gridlines and Rows and Column Headings to remove the Xs.)

DELETING A WORKSHEET OR GRAPH FROM A SLIDE

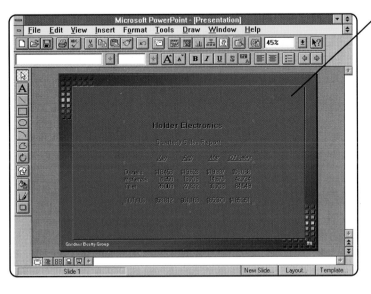

1. Click on the **worksheet** if it doesn't already have selection handles.

2. Press the **Backspace or Delete key**. The worksheet will be deleted from the slide.

USING THE EXCEL BUTTON IN THE TOOLBAR

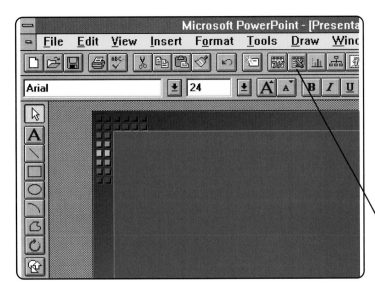

If you have Excel 5, you can call it up from within PowerPoint and use it to create a new worksheet. Excel 5 does not have to be running. This button will open it for you. (How efficient can you get!) Use a blank slide format for your slide.

1. Click on the **Insert Microsoft Excel Worksheet button** in the toolbar. A pull-down grid will appear.

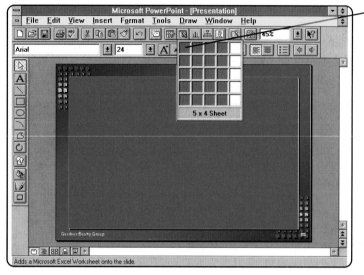

2. **Place** the mouse pointer on the **first square** in the grid.

3. **Press and hold** the mouse button and **drag** the pointer **across and down** to **indicate how many columns and rows** will be in your worksheet. The grid will expand as you drag. In this example, there are four columns and five rows. **Release** the mouse button when you have finished.

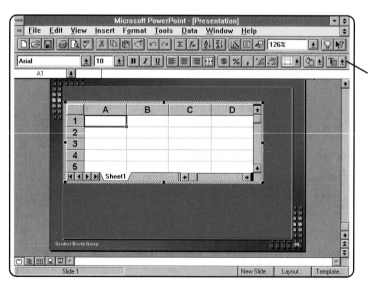

This worksheet will appear on your screen.

Notice that the toolbars have changed to Excel toolbars. Pretty amazing! You can create a worksheet just as you would in Excel with all the standard Excel formatting.

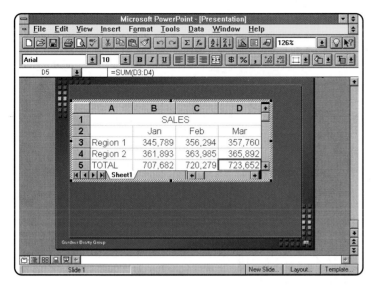

4. When you have completed the worksheet, **click anywhere off** the **worksheet** to insert it into the slide.

Then follow the previous steps on editing and enlarging the worksheet.

Quite honestly, we found this worksheet awkward to use. If you want to use a worksheet or graph in PowerPoint, we recommend that you follow the previous steps for importing an object. We found it much easier. You can, of course, copy and paste from any other Windows application into PowerPoint.

Working with Tables

PowerPoint has a predesigned slide that brings up a Word 6 table. There is also a button in the toolbar that will boot you into Word 6. In this chapter you will do the following:

❖ Use the predesigned Table slide
❖ Use the Insert Microsoft Word Table button

USING THE TABLE SLIDE

PowerPoint has a predesigned table slide that opens Word 6 and brings up a table. If you aren't familiar with Microsoft's Word 6 tables, refer to *Word for Windows 6: The Visual Learning Guide* for a more detailed discussion of how to create a table. If you don't have Word 6 installed on your computer, you will not be able to do these procedures.

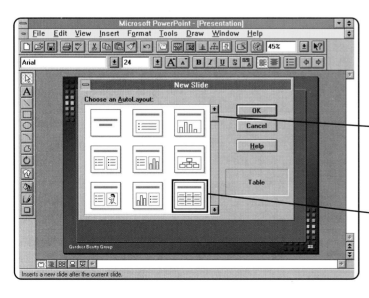

1. Click on the **New Slide button** at the bottom of your screen. This will bring up the New Slide dialog box you see here.

2. Press and hold the mouse button on the scroll button and **drag** it to the **top** of the **scroll bar**.

3. Click twice on the **Table slide**. It is the last slide in the third row. The Table slide will appear on your screen.

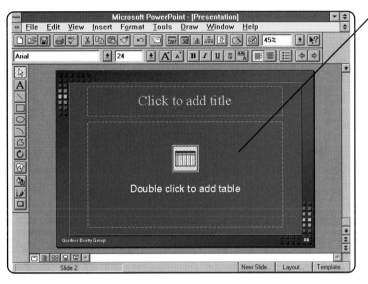

4. **Click twice** on the **table text block**. The Insert Word Table dialog box will appear.

Setting Up Columns and Rows

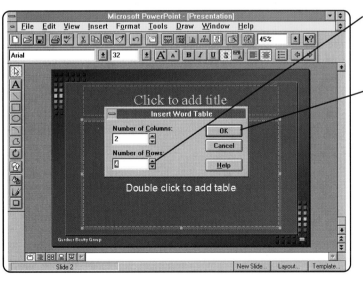

1. **Click twice** on ▲ to **increase** the number of rows to **4**.

2. **Click** on **OK**.

After a considerable hourglass intermission, a Word table will appear with two columns and four rows.

ENTERING TEXT IN THE TABLE

1. **Click** in the **first cell** of the table if the cursor is not already there.

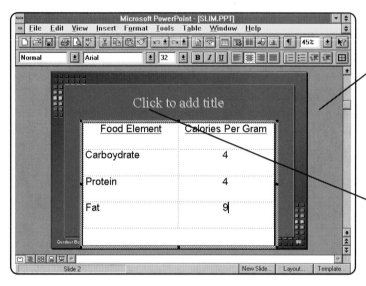

2. **Enter and format** the **text** as you would do in Word 6.

3. **Click** on the **background** to insert the table into the slide. It will appear without gridlines because you have to add them in Word 6 in order for them to show.

4. **Click** on the **title text block**.

5. **Type Comparison of Calories**.

EDITING A TABLE

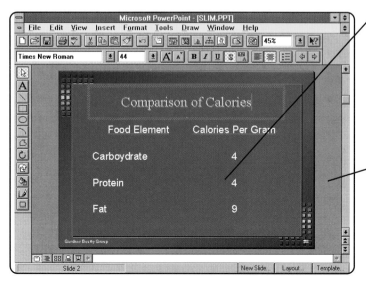

1. **Click twice** on the **table** in the slide. This will boot you back into the Word 6 table.

2. **Make** your **edits** as you would do in Word 6.

3. **Click anywhere** on the **background** to insert the edited table back into the slide.

USING THE WORD 6 BUTTON

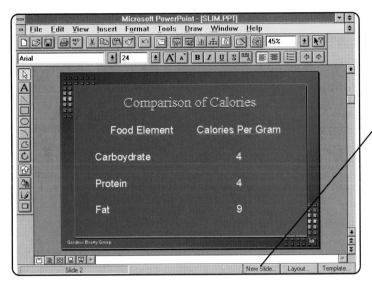

You have to have Word 6 installed on your computer in order to do this next section. First, you will add a blank slide.

1. Click on the **New Slide button** at the bottom of your screen The New Slide dialog box will appear.

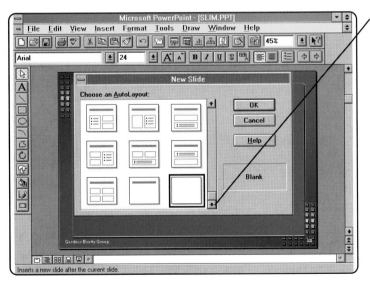

2. Press and hold the mouse button on the scroll button and **drag** it to the **bottom** of the **scroll bar**.

3. Click twice on the **blank slide**. A blank slide will appear on your screen.

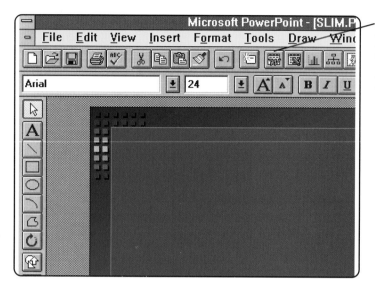

4. Click on the **Insert Microsoft Word Table button** in the toolbar. A pull-down grid will appear.

Setting Up the Table

1. Place the mouse pointer on the **first cell** of the grid.

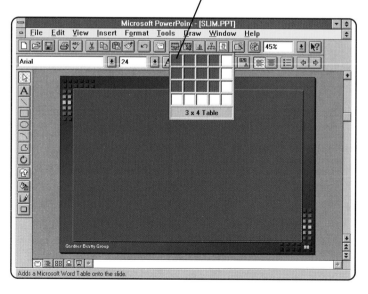

2. Press and hold the mouse button and **drag** the pointer **across and down** to **highlight** the **number of columns and rows** you want in the table. This example has four columns and three rows.

3. Release the mouse button when you have highlighted the appropriate number of squares. You will see the hourglass, and then a table will appear on your screen.

In this example, you will not actually enter any data into the table.

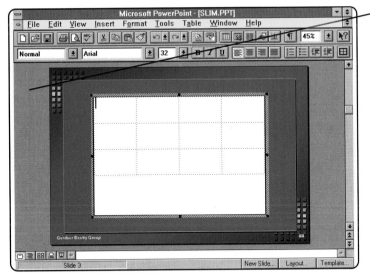

4. Click anywhere on the **background** to enter the table into the slide. Notice that the selection handles are the only thing you see on your screen. This is because you must add gridlines to a table in Word 6 in order for them to show.

In Chapter 15, "Creating an Organization Chart," you will add another new screen to this presentation.

Creating an Organization Chart

PowerPoint has a predesigned slide for an organization chart. You can customize it to show the organization chart of an entire company or project team. In this chapter you will do the following:

❖ Create an organization chart

❖ Change the format of the chart

USING THE ORG CHART SLIDE

In this section, you will add an organization chart to the new presentation you created in Chapters 12 and 13. If you want to create an overhead transparency, use Pick a Look Wizard and select Black and White Overheads. See Chapter 3, "Choosing a Predesigned Template," if you need help. This chapter will show the organization chart as a slide.

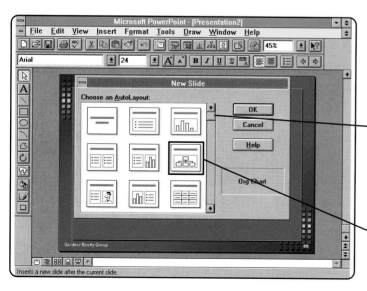

1. **Click** on the **New Slide button** at the bottom of your screen. This will bring up the New Slide dialog box that you see here.

2. **Move** the mouse arrow to the **scroll button** and **press and hold** the **button** and **drag** it to the **top** of the **scroll bar**.

3. **Click twice** on the **Org Chart slide**, which is the last slide in the second row.

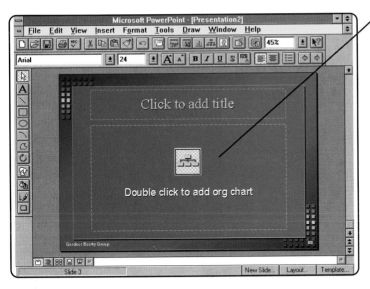

4. Click twice on the **org chart text block**. You will see an hourglass, and then the Microsoft Organization Chart window will appear. The boxes in the chart will be in the colors you previously selected for fill and lines. You will change the color of the fill and lines later in this chapter.

Enlarging the Window

You can enlarge the Organization Chart window to give yourself more work space.

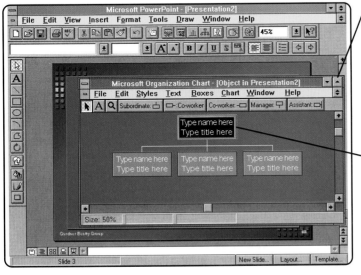

1. Click on the **Maximize button (▲)** on the right side of the Microsoft Organization Chart title bar. The window will be maximized and fill your screen.

2. After the window is maximized, **click inside** the **top box**. It will expand to show four lines.

ENTERING NAMES IN THE CHART

Each box has four lines you can use. The first two lines ("Type name here" and "Type title here") will print as you see them unless you enter data or hide the lines. The "<Comment>" lines will not print unless you enter data in them.

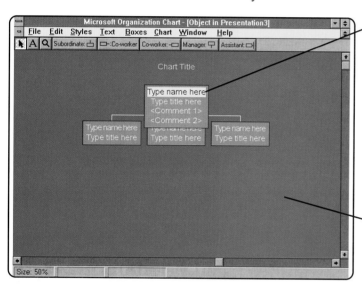

1. **Click** to the **left** of the **first line** and **drag** the cursor **over** the **text** to highlight it.

2. **Type Project Leader** and **press Enter**. The second line will be highlighted.

3. **Type TBA**.

4. **Click** on the **background** to close the box.

ADDING AN ASSISTANT

In this section, you will add an Assistant Project Leader.

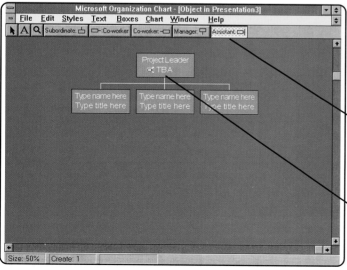

1. **Click** on the **Assistant button** in the toolbar. It will appear to be pressed in and lighter in color.

2. **Place** the cursor in the **Project Leader box**. The cursor will change to a box.

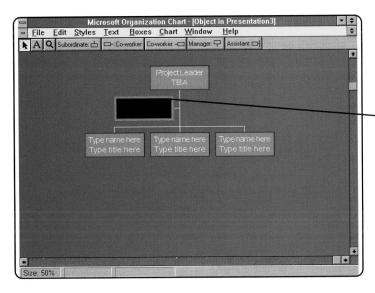

3. **Click** the mouse button.

A box will be added to the chart.

4. **Click** just **below** the top **border** of the box. It will be opened for editing and the first line will be highlighted.

5. **Type Asst. Proj. Leader**.

Hiding a Line

The first two lines in a box will print unless you enter text in them or hide them. In this example, you will hide the title line in the Assistant Project Leader box.

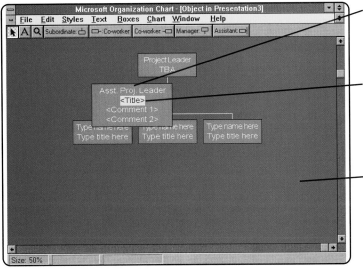

1. **Press the Enter** key to move to the second line and highlight it.

2. **Press** the **Delete key**. "<Title>" will appear. The angle brackets mean that this line will not print.

3. **Click** on the **background** to close the box.

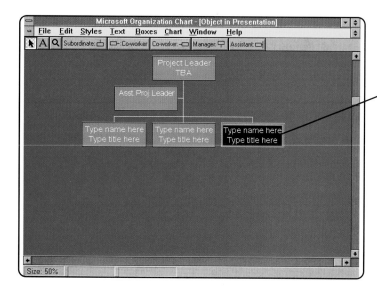

DELETING A BOX

1. Click on the **third box** in the **third line**. It will become black.

2. Press the **Delete key** on your keyboard. The box will be removed from the chart.

ADDING MANAGERS

In this example, you will add a Programming Manager and a Training Manager as direct reports to the project leader.

1. Click on this **box** to select it and make it black.

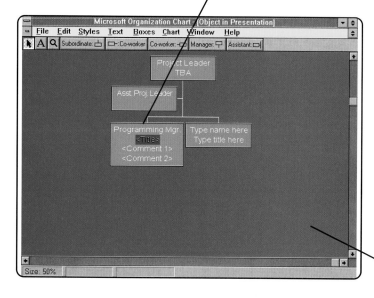

2. Click on the **box** a **second time** to open it for editing.

3. Highlight the **first line** and **type Programming Mgr**. Then **press Enter** to go to the second line and highlight it.

4. Press the **Delete key**. "<Title>" will appear, indicting that the line will not print.

5. Click on the **background** to close the box.

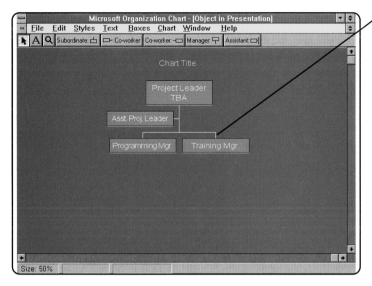

6. **Repeat steps 1 through 5** to insert "Training Mgr." in this box.

Notice that all the direct reports of the project leader (Asst. Proj. Leader and the Programming and Training managers) have only one line of type and have therefore become one line deep. If one of these boxes had two lines of type, all other boxes on the same level would have two lines.

ADDING SUBORDINATES

1. **Click** on the **Subordinate button** in the toolbar.

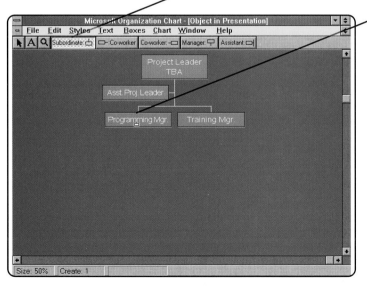

2. **Place** the mouse pointer in the **Programming Manager's box**. The pointer will become a box.

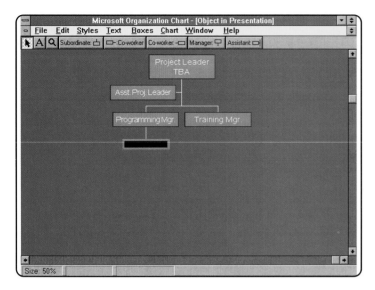

3. Click the **mouse button**.

A box will be added below the Programming Manager's box.

USING A COMMENT LINE

1. Click inside the **new box**. It will expand to show four lines. The first line will be highlighted.

2. Type Programmer.

3. Press Enter to move to the title line. Notice that it appears in angle brackets to indicate that it will not print. Each level takes its cue from the previous level. Because the previous level doesn't have a second line, this level doesn't have a second line either. (You can, of course, add text here if you want.)

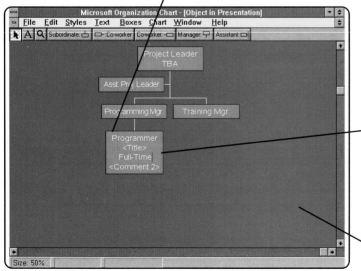

4. Press Enter to move to the first comment line and highlight it.

5. Type Full-Time.

6. Click on the **background** to close the box.

ADDING A CO-WORKER

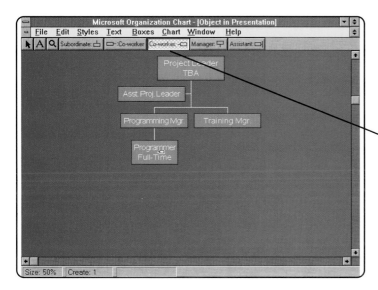

A co-worker can be added to any level of the chart. In this example, you will add a co-worker to the full-time programmer.

1. Click on the **right Co-worker button** in the toolbar.

2. Place the mouse pointer in the **Programmer's box**. The pointer will become a box.

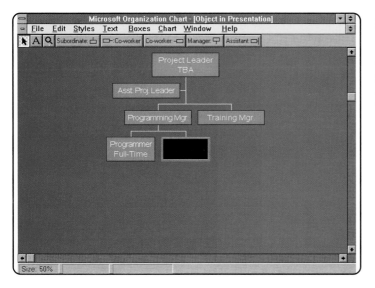

3. Click the **mouse button**.

A box will be added to the right of the full-time programmer.

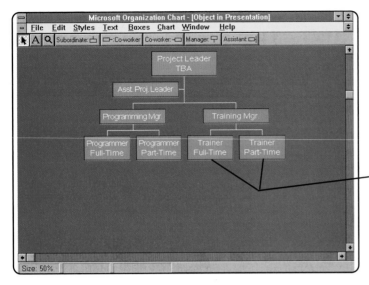

4. Repeat steps 1 through 5 in the section "Using a Comment Line" to type the following information in the co-worker's box:

Programmer

Part-Time.

5. Repeat the **steps** in the sections "Adding a Co-Worker" and "Using a Comment Line" to add the full- and part-time trainers you see here.

INSERTING THE ORGANIZATION CHART INTO YOUR PRESENTATION

1. Click on **File** in the menu bar. A pull-down menu will appear.

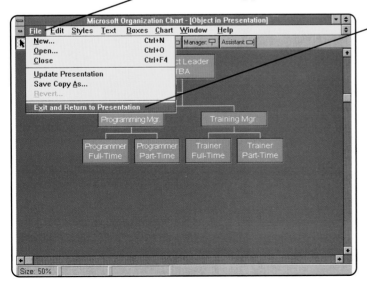

2. Click on **Exit and Return to Presentation**. The Microsoft Organization Chart dialog box will appear.

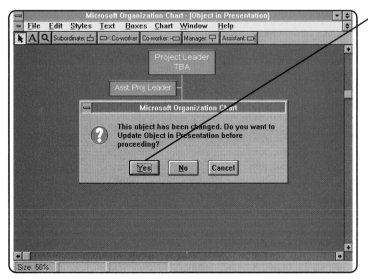

3. **Click** on **Yes**. The window will close and the organization chart will be inserted in the presentation slide.

EDITING THE ORGANIZATION CHART

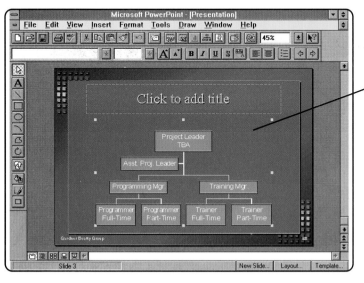

You can edit the chart even after it has been inserted into the presentation.

1. **Click twice** on the **chart**. The Microsoft Organization Chart window will appear.

2. **Click** on the **Maximize button** (▲) to increase the size of the window, as you did at the beginning of this chapter.

SELECTING ALL LEVELS

You can select all boxes on the chart and apply a command to all of them at one time.

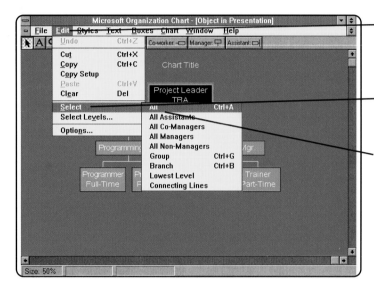

1. Click on **Edit** in the menu bar. A pull-down menu will appear.

2. Click on **Select**. A second menu will appear.

3. Click on **All**. All of the boxes will be selected.

Notice that you can select specific levels and the connecting lines.

CHANGING BOX COLOR

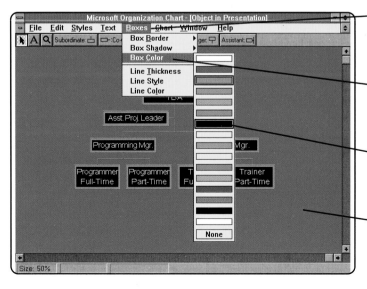

1. Click on **Boxes** in the menu bar. A pull-down menu will appear.

2. Click on **Box Color**. A pull-down color menu will appear.

3. Click on the **color you want** the boxes to be. In this example, it is black.

4. Click on the **background** to remove the selection borders so that you can see the boxes clearly.

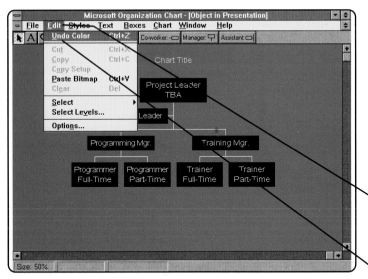

UNDOING A CHANGE

You can use the Undo feature to reverse the change you just made in the color if you use Undo before you do any other function.

1. **Click** on **Edit** in the menu bar. A pull-down menu will appear.

2. **Click** on **Undo Color**.

CHANGING THE STYLE OF THE CHART

You can change the style of the chart with a click of your mouse. In this example, you will reorganize around the managers.

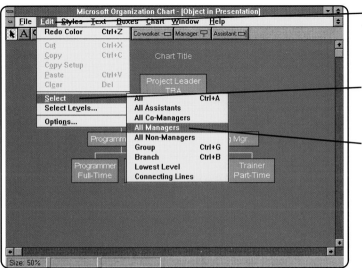

1. **Click** on **Edit** in the menu bar. A pull-down menu will appear.

2. **Click** on **Select**. A second menu will appear.

3. **Click** on **All Managers**. All levels that have direct reports will be highlighted.

4. Click on **Style** in the menu bar. A pull-down chart of Group styles will appear.

5. Click on the **style** of **chart** you want. In this example, click on the middle button in the top row to change to a vertical arrangement by managers.

If you change your mind, use Undo to go back to the previous chart setup.

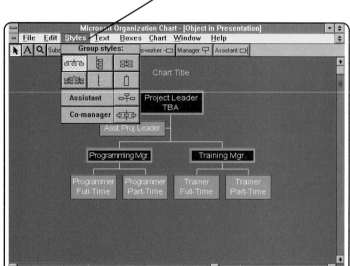

6. Click on **Edit** in the menu bar. A pull-down menu will appear.

7. Click on **Undo Chart Style**. Notice that PowerPoint knows that your last move was to change the chart.

8. Repeat the **steps** in the section "Inserting the Organization Chart into the Presentation," earlier in this chapter.

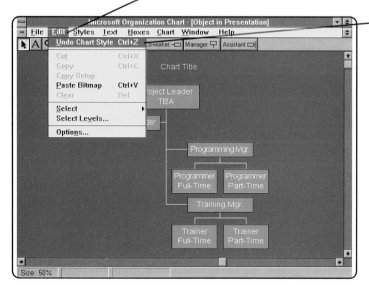

CLOSING A PRESENTATION WITHOUT SAVING

In Chapter 13, you opened a new presentation and created graphs, tables, and charts. Because this was only for practice, you don't need to save the presentation. In this section, you will close the new presentation without saving it.

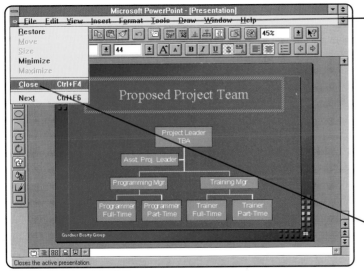

1. **Click** on the **control menu box** (⊟) on the left side of the menu bar. A pull-down menu will appear. This Control menu box controls this particular presentation. Be careful not to click on the top Control menu box. It controls the PowerPoint program.

2. **Click** on **Close**. A Microsoft PowerPoint dialog box will appear.

3. **Click** on **No** to close the presentation without saving it. You will be returned to the SLIM presentation at the same spot where you opened the new presenta-tion. If you want to save the presentation, click on Yes. The Save As dialog box will appear. Then follow the steps in Chapter 2 for naming and saving a file.

Program Manager

Part IV: Running a Slide Show

Setting Up and Rehearsing a Slide Show

PowerPoint provides exciting special effects and rehearsal tools to help make your presentations top-notch. In this chapter you will do the following:

❖ Add a black slide
❖ Apply and edit slide transitions
❖ Create a build slide
❖ Hide a slide
❖ Rehearse a slide show
❖ Run a slide show

ADDING A BLACK SLIDE

A black slide at the end of a presentation focuses the audience's attention back on the speaker. This is useful for both a 35 mm slide presentation and an electronic presentation.

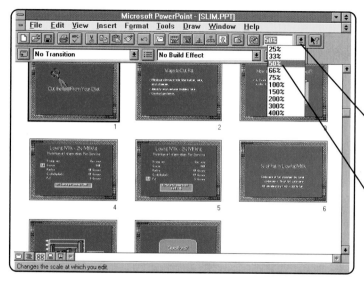

1. **Click** on the **Slide Sorter View button** at the bottom of your screen to go to Slide Sorter view.

2. **Click** on the ⬇ next to the Zoom Control box. A drop-down menu will appear.

3. **Click on 50%**. The slides will appear in a 50 percent view, and you will be able to see all the slides at one time.

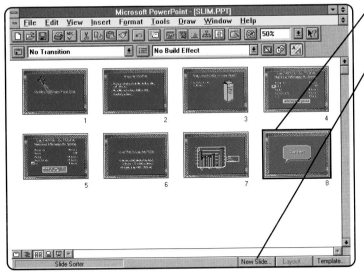

4. **Click** on **slide 8** to select it.

5. **Click** on **New Slide**. The New Slide dialog box will appear.

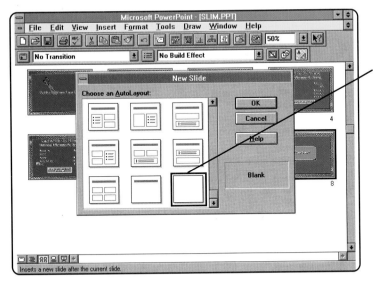

6. **Scroll down** until you can see the Blank slide.

7. **Click twice** on the **Blank slide**. A blank slide will be added to your presentation.

Removing Background Elements from a Slide

To color this slide entirely black, you have to remove the background elements that are part of the Pick a Look Wizard template.

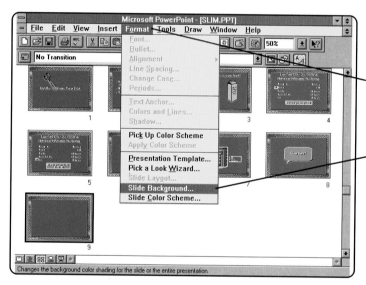

1. Click on **slide 9** if it is not already selected.

2. Click on **Format** in the menu bar. A pull-down menu will appear.

3. Click on **Slide Background**. The Slide Background dialog box will appear.

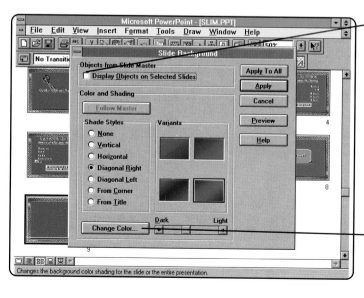

4. Click on **Display Objects on Selected Slides** to remove the X. This will remove the design objects from the slide.

Changing the Background Color

1. Click on **Change Color**. The Background Color dialog box will appear.

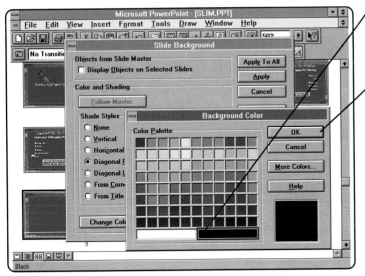

2. Click on the color **black** at the bottom of the dialog box.

3. Click on **OK**. The Slide Background dialog box will reappear.

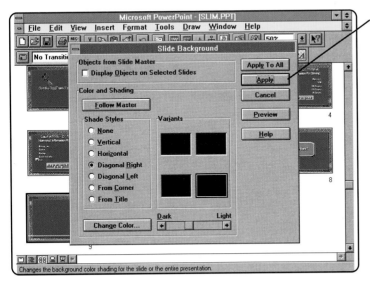

4. Click on **Apply**. The Slide Sorter view will appear with a black slide 9.

APPLYING A
SLIDE TRANSITION

If you run your slide show on your computer, one very impressive special effect you can add is slide transitions. Slide transitions determine how one slide fades or dissolves into the next. You can apply transitions to individual slides, multiple slides, or all the slides at once.

Using Select All

1. Click on **Edit** in the menu bar. A pull-down menu will appear.

2. Click on **Select All**. The Slide Sorter view will appear with all the slides in your presentation selected.

Selecting a
Slide Transition

There are over 40 transition effects from which to choose. In this section, you will choose a Random Transition effect.

1. Click on **Tools** in the menu bar. A pull-down menu will appear.

2. Click on **Transition**. The Transition dialog box will appear.

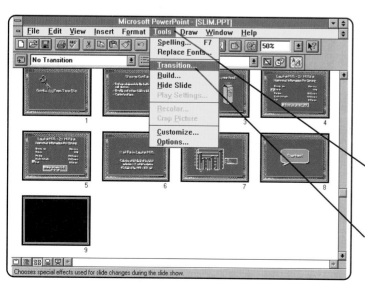

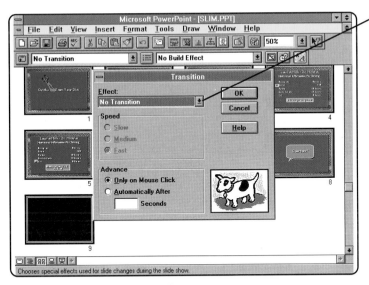

3. **Click** on the ↓ next to the Effect box. A drop-down list will appear.

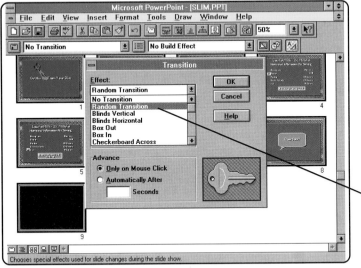

4. **Press** the ↓ on your keyboard to scroll through the list of transitions.Notice that an example of the effect is shown in the lower right corner of the dialog box. When you've seen the last transition, **scroll up** to the top of the list.

5. **Click** on **Random Transition**. The drop-down list will disappear.

Selecting a Transition Speed and Advance

You can control the speed of slide transitions. You can also decide if you want your slides to advance automatically or when you click your mouse.

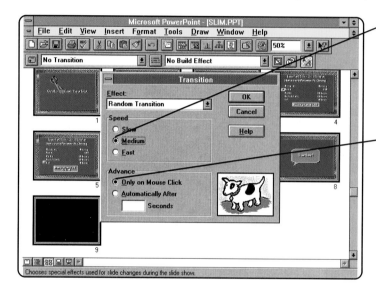

1. **Click** on **Medium** to put a dot in the circle. An example of this transition speed will appear in the display box.

2. **Click** on **Only on Mouse Click** to put a dot in the circle.

3. **Click** on **OK**. The Slide Sorter view will appear.

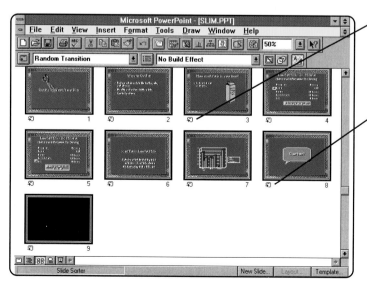

Notice the symbol that appears underneath the slides, indicates that a transition has been applied.

4. **Click** on **one** of the **transition symbols**. An example of the transition that is applied to the slide will be displayed. Pretty neat!

USING SLIDE SHOW VIEW

Slide Show view allows you to preview the transitions you have applied.

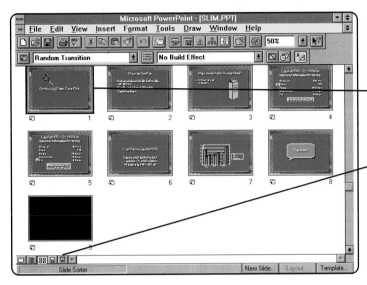

1. **Click** on the **white space** on the screen to deselect all the slides.

2. **Click** on **slide 1** to select it. The slide show starts with the active slide.

3. **Click** on the **Slide Show button**, which is the last button at the bottom of your screen. After a pause, the first slide in your presentation will appear.

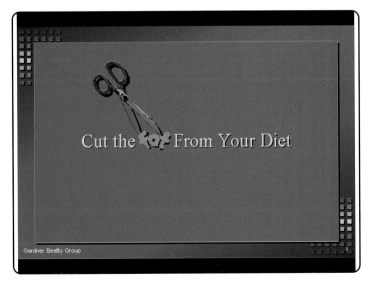

4. **Click** your **mouse or press** the **Page Down key** to go to slide 2. Notice the transition effect.

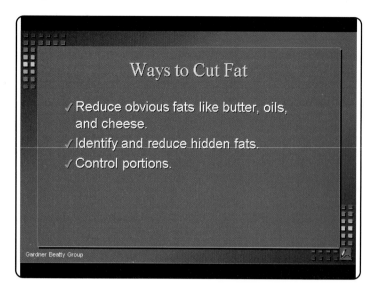

5. **Click or press** the **Page Down key** to move to **slide 3**.

6. **Continue** to **click** to move to the **next slide until** you reach the **last slide** in your presentation.

7. **Click or press** the **Page Down key**. The Slide Sorter view will appear.

Note: You can press the Esc key at any time during the presentation to exit the Slide Show view.

EDITING TRANSITIONS BETWEEN SLIDES

After previewing your slide show, you may want to change some of the transitions. It's very easy to edit a slide transition.

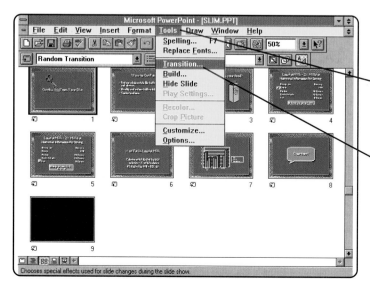

1. **Click** on **slide 1** or the slide you want to edit.

2. **Click** on **Tools** in the menu bar. A pull-down menu will appear.

3. **Click** on **Transition**. The Transition dialog box will appear.

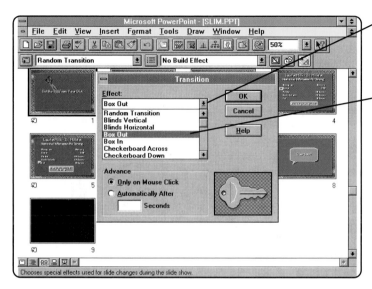

4. **Click** on the ⬇ next to the Effect box. A drop-down list will appear.

5. **Click** on **Box Out** or a transition you prefer. The drop-down list will disappear, and a sample of the transition will be displayed.

6. **Click** on **Slow** to put a dot in the circle. An example of this transition speed will appear in the display box.

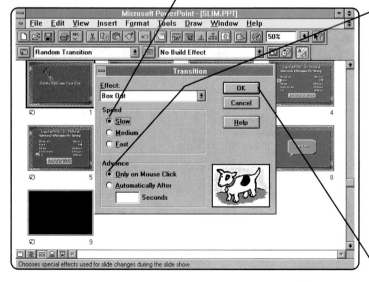

7. **Click** on **Only on Mouse Click** to put a dot in the circle.

Notice that you can also select Automatically After and specify a time so that the next slide in your presentation will appear automatically. You will learn how to automate your presentation later in this chapter.

8. **Click** on **OK**.

REMOVING TRANSITIONS

You can remove transitions completely if you wish.

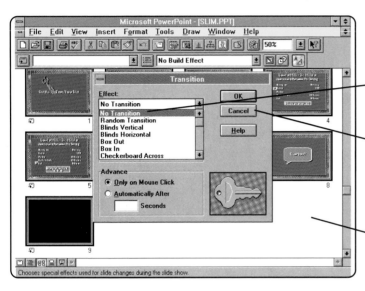

1. **Select all** the **slides** and **open** the **Transition dialog box**. See "Applying a Slide Transition" earlier in this chapter if you need help.

2. **Click** on **No Transition** in the Effect box.

3. If you are following the steps in this chapter, **click** on **Cancel**. Or **click** on **OK** to remove all transitions.

4. **Click** on the **white space** to deselect the slides.

CREATING A BUILD SLIDE

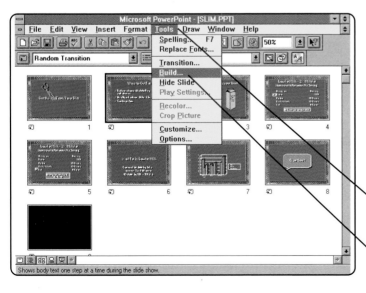

A *build slide* is another exciting effect that can be used when you show your slide show on a computer. A build slide allows you to reveal bulleted points on a slide one at a time.

1. **Click** on **slide 2** to select it.

2. **Click** on **Tools** in the menu bar.

3. **Click** on **Build**. The Build dialog box will appear.

4. Click on **Build Body Tex**t to insert an X in the box.

Choosing a Color for Dimmed Bullets

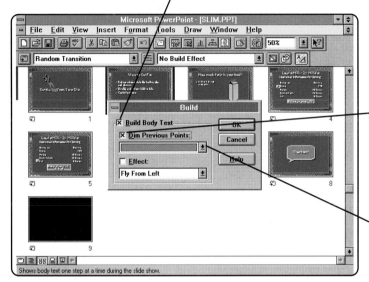

When a second bulleted item appears on the screen, you can make the first item dimmer in color.

1. Click on **Dim Previous Points** to insert an X in the box. This is the color that will be used for dimmed points unless you change it.

2. Click on the ⬇ next to the color box. A color menu will appear.

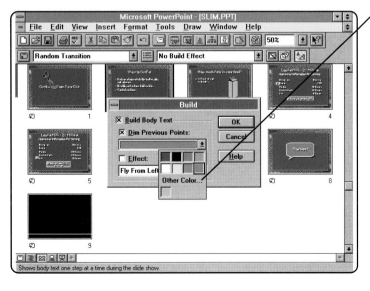

3. Click on **Other Color**. The Other Color dialog box will appear.

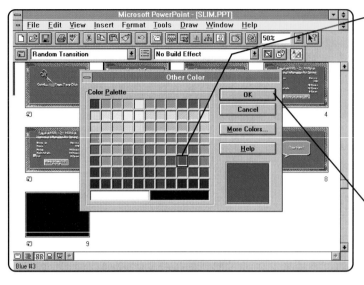

4. Click on **Blue #3**. It is in the third row from the bottom, three over from the right. An example of the color will appear in the lower right corner of the dialog box. And its name will appear at the very bottom of your screen.

5. Click on **OK**. The Build dialog box will reappear.

Choosing the Transition Effect for Bulleted Items

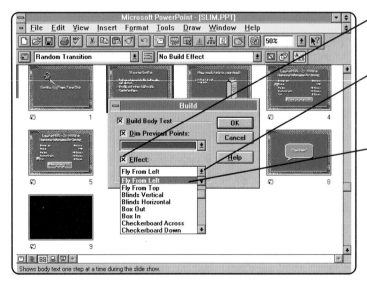

1. Click on **Effect** to insert an X in the box.

2. Click on the ⬇ next to the effect box. A drop-down list will appear.

3. Click on **Fly From Left** if it is not already selected.

4. Click on **OK**. The Build dialog box will disappear.

Notice the symbol resembling a bulleted list that appears below slide 2. This indicates that this is a build slide. You will learn how to display this effect later in this chapter.

USING THE HIDE SLIDE BUTTON

Hidden slides are set up so that you have the choice of including or not including them during a presentation.

Hiding a Slide

In this example, you will make slide 7 a hidden slide.

1. **Click** on **slide 7** to select it.

2. **Click** on the **Hide Slide button** in the toolbar. It is the third button from the right. It will appear pressed in and lighter in color.

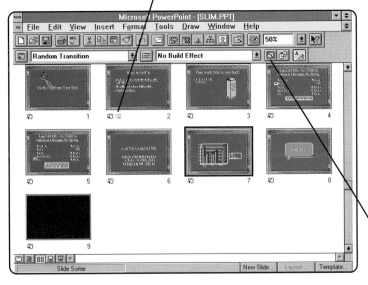

Notice the hidden slide symbol that appears below slide 7. You will learn how to use a hidden slide later in this chapter.

Removing the Hide Slide Option

The Hide Slide button works like a toggle switch. Click once to turn it on. Click again to turn it off.

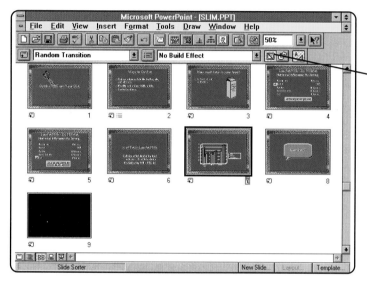

1. Click on **slide 7** if it is not already selected.

2. Click on the **Hide slide button**. The hidden slide symbol will disappear.

3. Click on the **Hide Slide button** once more to make slide 7 a hidden slide again.

REHEARSING A PRESENTATION

PowerPoint has several nifty tools to help you practice your presentation.

The Rehearse timings feature lets you time how long you spend on an individual slide or the entire presentation. You can then record the times and use them in the "Slide timings" advance option when you run your slide show. The slides will then advance automatically at the predetermined times.

Using the Rehearse Timings Button

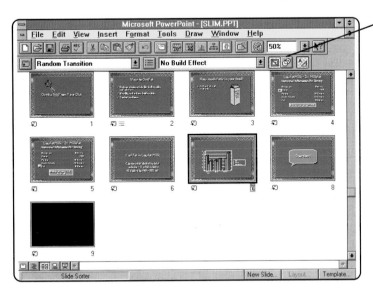

1. **Click** on the **Rehearse Timings button**. It is the second button from the right. Slide 1 will appear in Slide Show view. The Rehearse Timings button always starts at slide 1 regardless of which slide is selected.

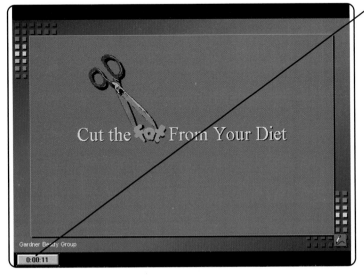

Notice the timer that appears in the lower left corner of your screen.

2. **Rehearse** what you plan to say for this slide.

3. **Click** your **mouse or press** the **Page Down key** when you are done with this slide. The timer will stop for slide 1 and begin at 0:00 for slide 2.

Displaying a Build Slide

Notice that only the title of the slide shows when a build slide first appears. In the rehearse timings mode, you have to click to bring up each bulleted item. The timing device will record a total time for the slide. If you later use the automatic timed advance feature, PowerPoint will divide the total time on the slide by the number of bullets to show each bullet.

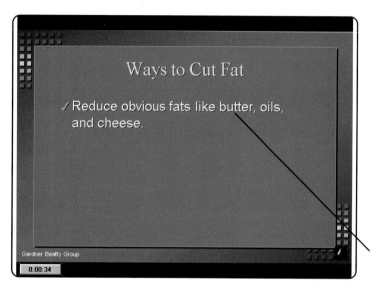

1. Click once on **slide 2** to bring the first bullet into view.

Notice that the text of the first bullet is bright.

2. Click once on **slide 2** to bring the second bullet onto the slide.

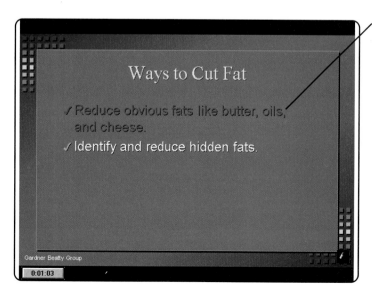

Notice that the first bullet is dimmed and the second bullet is now bright.

3. Click once again on **slide 2** to bring the third bullet into view.

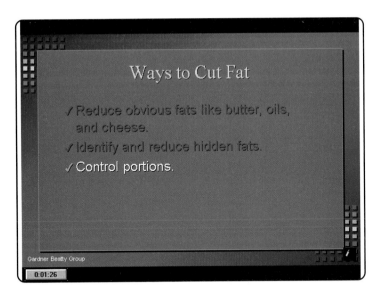

Notice that the first two bullets are dimmed and the third is now the bright bullet.

4. Click your **mouse or press** the **Page down key** to go to slide 3. The timer will stop for slide 2 and begin at 0:00 for slide 3.

5. Click to show **slides 3, 4, 5, and 6**. Slide 6 will appear on your screen, as shown in the example below.

Using the Annotation Tool

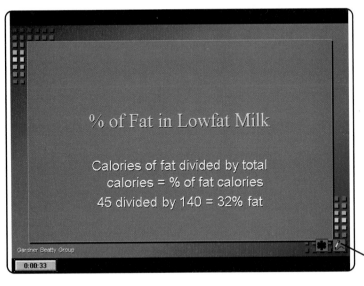

Notice the two symbols in the bottom right corner of your screen.

The symbol that looks like a pencil is a drawing or annotation tool.

The symbol that looks like a shamrock indicates that there is a hidden slide after this slide.

1. Click on the **Annotation tool**. Don't panic if you can't see your mouse pointer when you try to move to the bottom of the screen. In this mode, your mouse pointer may not be visible when it is moving. You'll be able to see it when you stop the mouse.

Notice that your pointer now has the shape of a pencil and that the annotation symbol is "storing" your arrow for you. This tells you that the annotation tool is now active.

2. **Place** the mouse pointer **where you want to begin** drawing or writing on your slide.

3. **Press and hold** your mouse button **and underline "32% fat." Release** the mouse button.

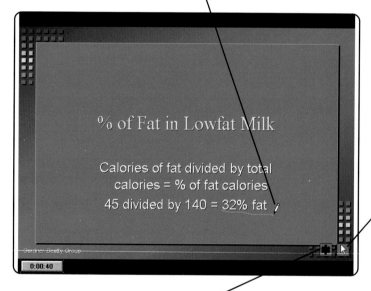

If you feel like you're in kindergarten when you first use this tool, practicing will make it go more smoothly.

The marks you make on the slide during annotation mode are only temporary. After you change slides, they will disappear.

4. **Click** on the **mouse pointer** being stored at the bottom of your screen to exit the annotation mode.

Revealing a Hidden Slide

You have two options with a hidden slide. You can skip slide 7 by clicking your mouse or you can click on the hidden slide symbol and reveal slide 7. In this example, you will reveal the hidden slide.

1. **Click** on the **hidden slide symbol**.

Notice that the hidden slide shows a timer in the corner. If you had chosen not to reveal the hidden slide, it would not have had a time applied to it. It would have remained a manual slide. This might be an option to consider during your presentation.

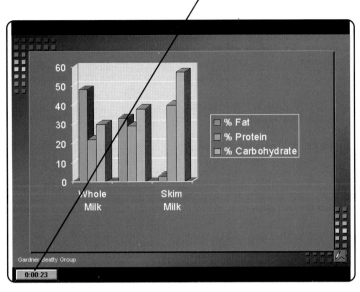

2. Click your **mouse or press** the **Page Down key** to go to the next slide. The timer will start at 0:00 for this slide.

3. Repeat step 2 for the remaining slides in your presentation. A Microsoft PowerPoint dialog box will appear after you have clicked on the last slide in your presentation.

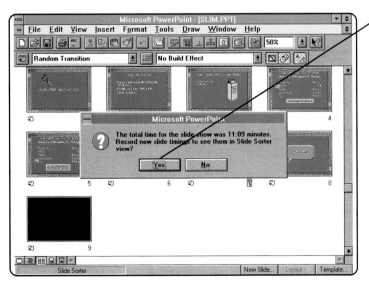

4. Click on **Yes** if you are happy with your rehearsal **or click** on **No** and the new times will not be applied. You will return to Slide Sorter view.

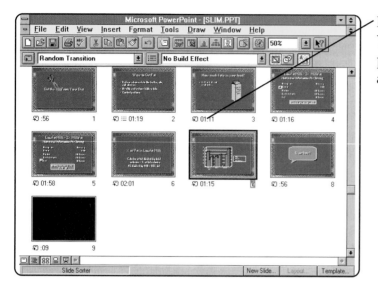

Notice that if you clicked on Yes in the previous step, the practice times have been applied to your slides.

RUNNING A SLIDE SHOW

There are two ways to start your slide show.

Using the View Menu

1. **Click** on **View** in the menu bar. A pull-down menu will appear.

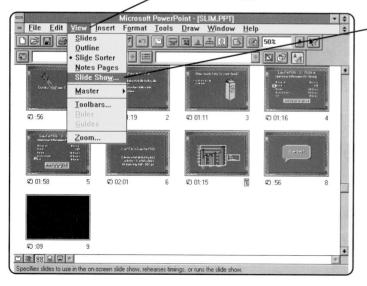

2. **Click** on **Slide Show**. The Slide Show dialog box will appear.

You can either select all of the slides in your presentation or a range of slides.

You can select Manual Advances. This allows you to run your slides manually without erasing the times you have set for an automatic slide show.

Select Use Slide Timings to run your slide show with the existing slide times.

If you are unhappy with your slide times, you can Rehearse New timings.

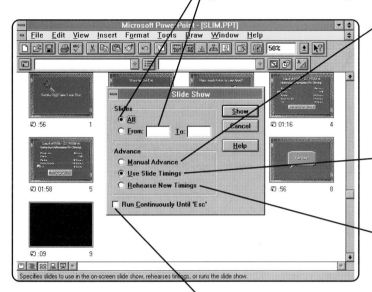

An exciting PowerPoint feature is the ability to run an automatic slide show continuously. This is a wonderful option to use in a display booth.

Choose your slides and Advance by clicking on the options of your choice. In this example, you will select All and Use Slide Timings.

3. Click on **All** if it is not already selected.

4. Click on **Use Slide Timings**.

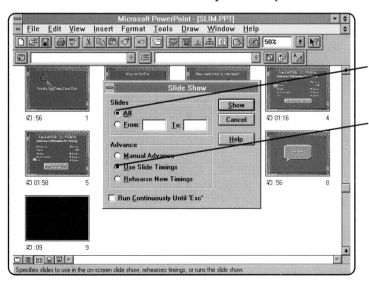

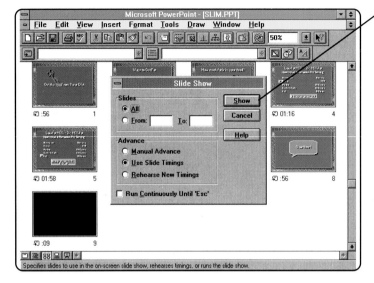

5. **Click** on **Show**. After a pause, your slide show presentation will begin.

Practice your slide show or press the Esc key to return to Slide Sorter view if you don't wish to view your entire presentation.

Now that you're a pro at presenting your slide show, "break a leg," as they say in the theater.

Taking Your Show on the Road

If you want to take or send a presentation off-site and show it on a computer, there are a few things you should do first. In this chapter you will do the following:

❖ Save your presentation with embedded fonts

❖ Copy the PowerPoint Viewer diskette

❖ Learn how to run a presentation on a computer that doesn't have PowerPoint

SAVING A PRESENTATION WITH EMBEDDED FONTS

If you show your presentation on another computer that does not have the same fonts you used in your slides, your presentation may look different. Power-Point allows you to embed your presentation's fonts into the presentation. When you view the presentation on another computer, it will look exactly as you created it, regardless of whether the new computer has the same fonts.

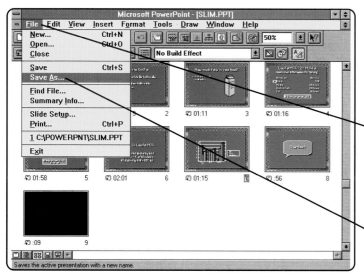

1. **Open slim.ppt** to **Slide Sorter view** if it is not already open.

2. **Click** on **File** in the menu bar. A pull-down menu will appear. It doesn't matter what view you're in when you do this.

3. **Click** on **Save As**. The Save As dialog box will appear.

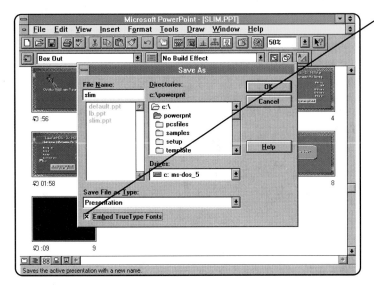

4. **Click** on **Embed True Type Fonts** to insert an ✕ into the box. (Only True Type fonts can be embedded. Keep this in mind when you design a slide show that you know will be sent out of the office.)

Saving a File to a Diskette

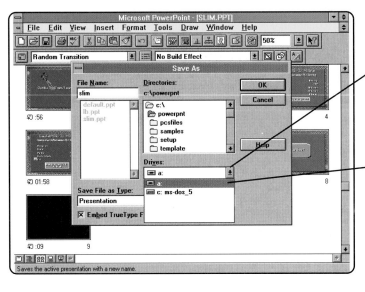

1. **Insert** a **formatted diskette** into drive a: (or b:).

2. While you are in the Save As dialog box, **click** on the ⬇ next to the Drives box. A drop-down list will appear.

3. **Click** on drive **a:** (or b:).

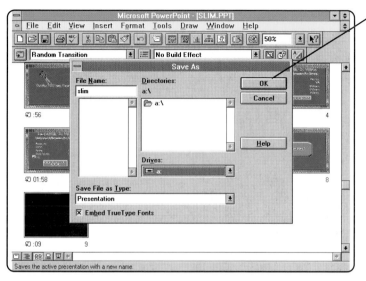

4. Click on **OK**. An hourglass will appear. Your file will be saved with embedded fonts, and the Summary Info dialog box will appear. If for some reason a font cannot be embedded, an alert will appear. Keep in mind that embedded fonts will increase the size of the file.

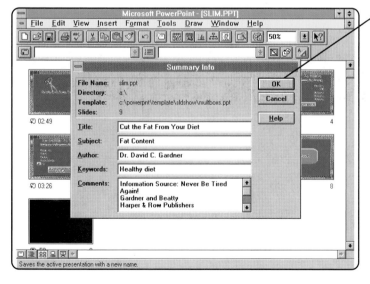

5. Click on **OK**.

6. Remove the **disk** containing the **embedded copy** of slim.ppt. You will use it later in this chapter.

VIEWING A SLIDE SHOW WHEN PowerPoint ISN'T AVAILABLE

If you take or send your presentation off-site, other computers may not have PowerPoint. Instead of installing PowerPoint, you can bring or send a copy of the PowerPoint Viewer, which is disk 12 of the Installation disks. The PowerPoint Viewer can be freely distributed, without any additional license.

Copying PowerPoint Viewer

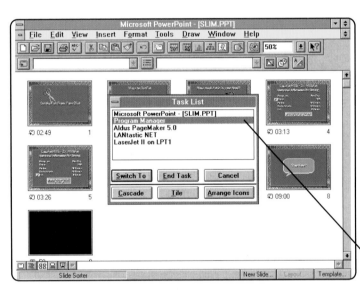

1. Press and hold the **Ctrl key** and **press** the **Esc key** (Ctrl + Esc). The Task List dialog box will appear.

2. Click twice on **Program Manager**. The Program Manager will appear.

3. Click twice on the Program group that contains **File Manager**.

4. Click twice on the **File Manager icon**. File Manager will appear.

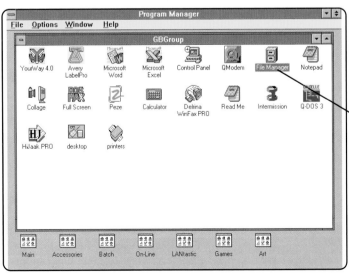

5. **Click** on **Disk** in the menu bar. A pull-down menu will appear.

6. **Click** on **Copy Disk**. The Copy Disk dialog box will appear.

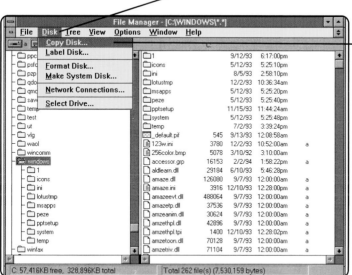

7. **Confirm** that both the Source In and Destination In boxes have A: (or B:) as the drive.

8. **Click on OK**. The confirm Copy Disk dialog box will appear.

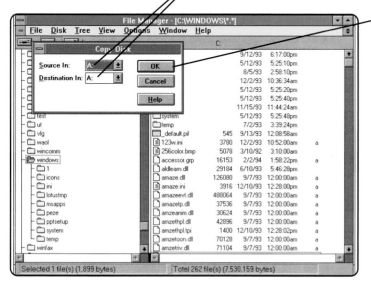

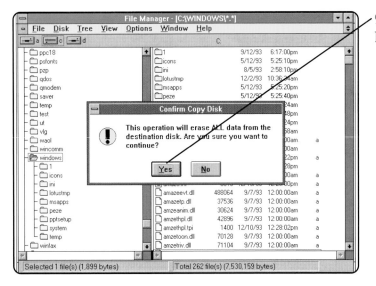

9. **Click** on **Yes**. The Copy Disk dialog box will appear.

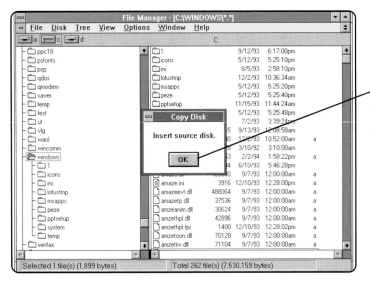

10. **Insert** your **source disk** (PowerPoint Viewer disk 12) into drive A (or B).

11. **Click** on **OK**. Another Copy Disk dialog box will appear.

The copying Disk dialog box shows you the percent completed as File Manager copies the disk. When the copying of the source disk is complete, a Copy Disk dialog box will appear.

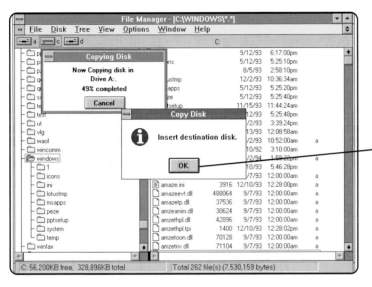

12. Remove the **source disk** from drive A (or B).

13. Insert a **blank, 1.44MB or 1.2MB floppy** into **drive A** (or B).

14. Click on **OK**.

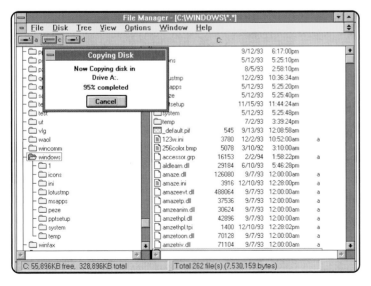

When the disk has been copied, the Copying Disk dialog box will disappear and you will be returned to File Manager.

15. **Click** on **File** in the menu bar. A pull-down menu will appear.

16. **Click** on **Exit**. File Manager will close.

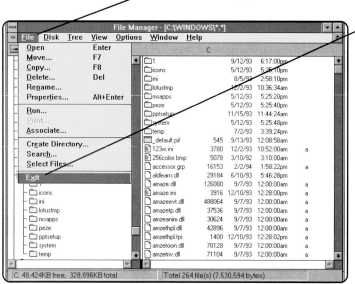

Installing the Viewer on the Host Computer

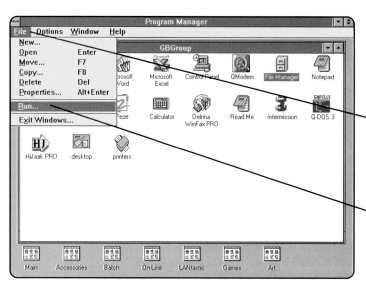

1. **Insert** the **copy** of the **Viewer disk** into the floppy drive of the computer that doesn't have PowerPoint.

2. **Click** on **File** in the menu bar of Program Manager. A pull-down menu will appear.

3. **Click** on **Run**. The Run dialog box will appear.

4. **Type a:\vsetup** (or b).

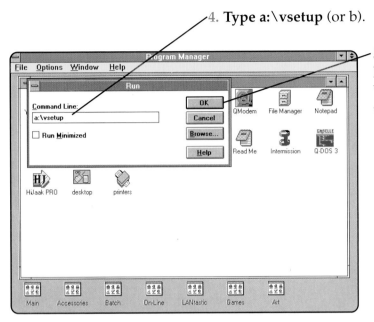

5. **Click** on **OK**. The Microsoft PowerPoint Viewer 4.0 Setup dialog box will appear.

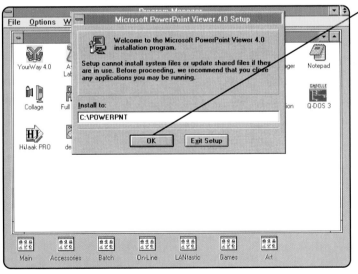

6. **Click** on **OK**.

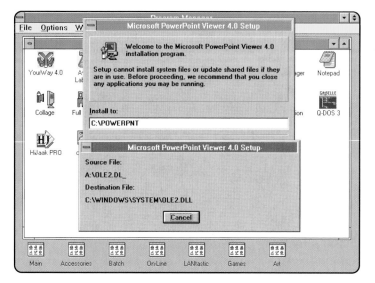

Sit back for a few minutes while the PowerPoint Viewer files are copied to the computer hard drive.

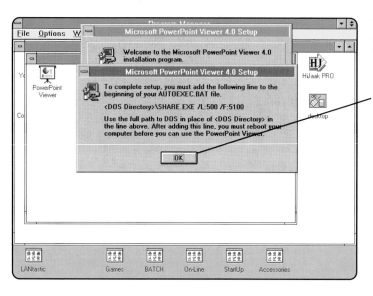

You may get the message you see in this example to the left.

7. **Click** on **OK**.

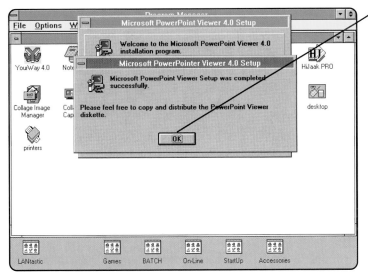

8. **Click** on **OK**. The PowerPoint Viewer is now installed. Remove the disk from drive a: (or b:)

You may get a message telling you to reboot Windows. After you have restarted Windows, the Microsoft Office group with the Viewer icon in it will appear.

Copying Your Presentation to a Hard Drive

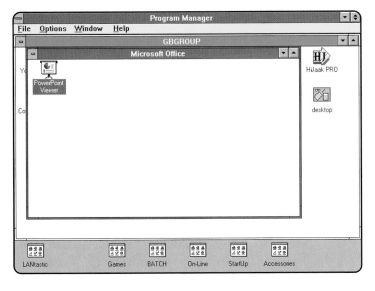

The presentation must be run from a hard drive in order to handle the transitions.

1. **Insert** the **disk** that has your PowerPoint file on it into drive a: (or b:).

2. **Go to** the Program group that contains **File Manager**.

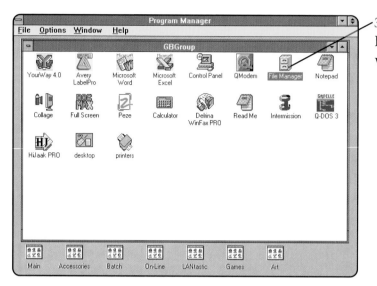

3. **Click twice** on the **file Manager icon**. File Manager will appear.

4. **Click** on **File** in the menu bar. A pull-down menu will appear.

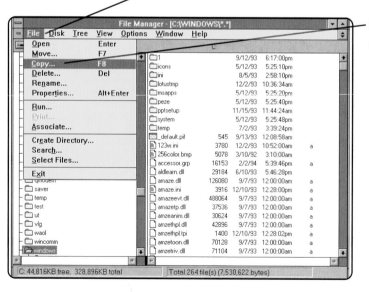

5. **Click** on **Copy**. The Copy dialog box will appear.

6. **Click twice** on the **Form box** to highlight the text in it.

7. **Type a:\slim.ppt** (or the name of your presentation.)

8. **Press** the **Tab key** to go to the To box.

9. **Type c:\powerpnt** (or the name of the directory where you want the file to go on the hard drive.)

10. **Click** on **OK**. The file will be copied to the hard drive.

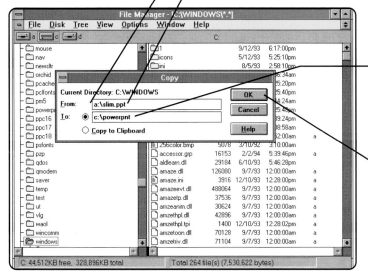

11. **Click twice** on the **Control menu box** (☐) to exit File Manager.

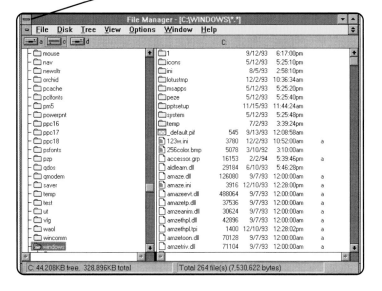

RUNNING A PRESENTATION IN THE POWERPOINT VIEWER

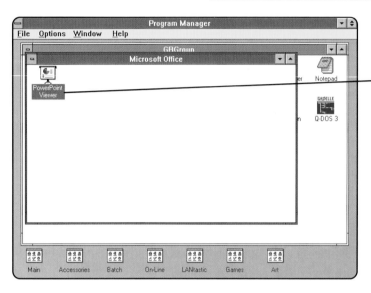

1. Go to the **Microsoft Office group**.

2. Click twice on the **PowerPoint Viewer icon**. The Microsoft PowerPoint Viewer dialog box will appear.

3. Click twice on the **powerpnt directory** or the name of the directory that contains your file.

4. Click on **slim.ppt** or the filename of your presentation.

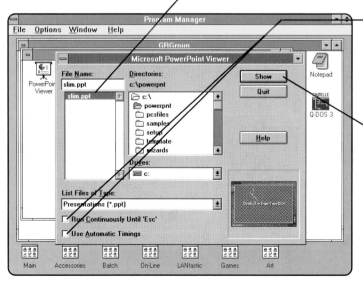

5. If you want to run your slide show continuously, **click** on **Run Continuously Until "Esc"** and **Use Automatic Timings**.

6. Click on **Show** when you are ready to begin. The Slide Show view will appear.

Program Manager

Part V: Special Features

Using Auto-Content Wizard

If you're unsure about how to begin a new presentation, use the AutoContent Wizard. PowerPoint has six presentation formats that include such topics as presenting a strategy, training, and reporting bad news. After you select a topic, AutoContent Wizard gives you a content-related outline that can be edited to fit your specific situation. The outline can then be turned into slides with a mouse click. In this chapter you will do the following:

❖ Use the AutoContent Wizard

❖ Work in Outline view

SELECTING AN AutoContent PRESENTATION

Begin AutoContent Wizard with a new presentation.

1. **Click** on **File** in the menu bar. A pull-down menu will appear.

2. **Click** on **New**. The New Presentation dialog box will appear.

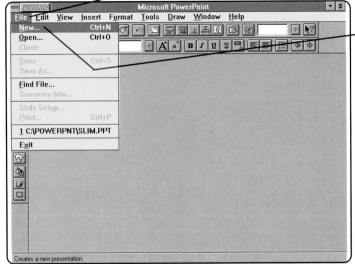

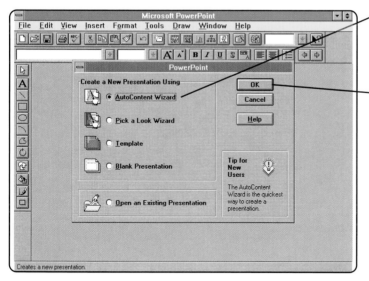

3. **Click** on **AutoContent Wizard** to put a dot in the circle.

4. **Click** on **OK**. The AutoContent Wizard - Step 1 of 4 dialog box will appear.

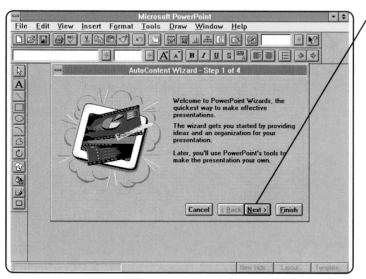

5. **Click** on **Next**. The AutoContent Wizard - Step 2 of 4 dialog box will appear.

Notice that your cursor is already flashing in the subject text box.

6. **Type** the **topic** of your presentation. You can, however, leave this blank and change it later.

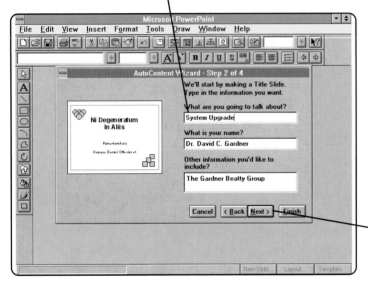

The name and company information that was used during the installation process will appear in the name and other information text boxes.

7. **Press** the **Tab key** to move to the name and other information text boxes to edit the information if necessary.

8. **Click** on **Next>**. The AutoContent Wizard - Step 3 of 4 dialog box will appear.

There are six different types of presentations in the AutoContent Wizard. As you click on a choice, an outline will appear in the display box on the left.

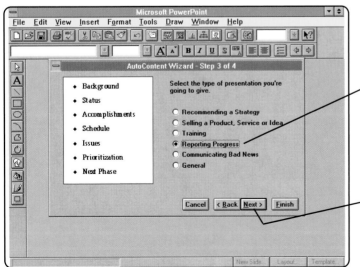

9. **Click** on the **presentation** that best approximates your slide show objective. In this example, it is Reporting Progress.

10. **Click** on **Next>**. The AutoContent Wizard - Step 4 of 4 dialog box will appear.

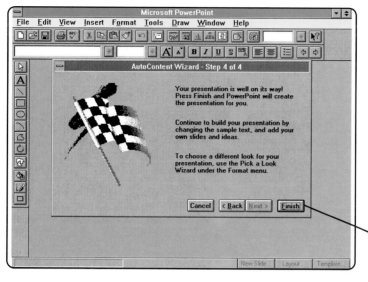

If you change your mind at any point while you are in the AutoContent Wizard, you can click on the <Back button to go to previous screens. After you click on the finish button, however, you will have to start the AutoContent Wizard over to choose a different presentation outline.

11. **Click** on **Finish**. After a pause, the presentation you selected will appear on your screen in Outline view.

MOVING A CUE CARD

When the presentation outline first appears, you may see a Cue Card dialog box to the right of the outline.

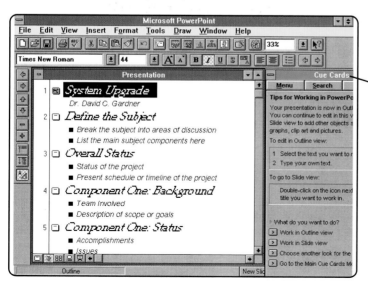

You can move the dialog box so that you can see it more clearly.

1. **Place** the mouse pointer on the **Cue Card title bar**.

2. **Press and hold** the mouse button and drag the dialog box away from the edge of the screen.

3. **Release** the mouse button when the dialog box is positioned where you want it.

Turning Off Cue Cards in AutoContent Wizard

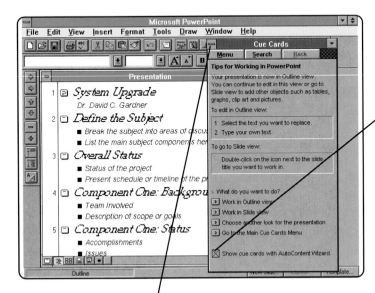

The Cue Cards dialog box will appear every time you use AutoContent Wizard, unless you turn it off.

1. Click on **Show cue cards with AutoContent Wizard** to *remove* the × from the box.

Closing the Cue Cards Dialog Box

1. Click twice on the **Control menu box** (⊟) on the left of the Cue Cards title bar. The dialog box will close.

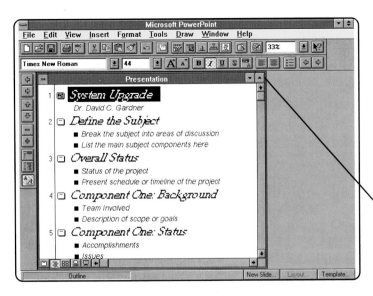

ENLARGING THE PRESENTATION WINDOW

If your Presentation window does not fill your screen, as you see in this example, you can enlarge it very easily.

1. Click on the ▲ (Maximize button) on the right of the Presentation title bar. The Presentation window will be enlarged.

WORKING IN OUTLINE VIEW

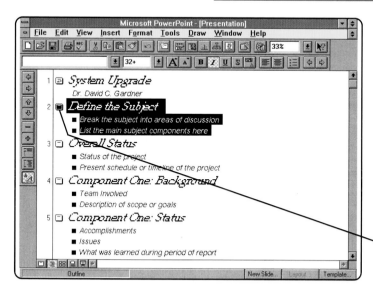

AutoContent Wizard appears in Outline view. You can, of course, switch to Slide view. In this section, you will delete a slide in Outline view.

Deleting a Slide in Outline View

1. **Click** on the **symbol beside slide 2**. All of the text in slide 2 will be highlighted.

2. **Press** the **Delete** (or Backspace) **key** on your keyboard. The highlighted text will be deleted and the remaining slides renumbered.

Editing Text in Outline View

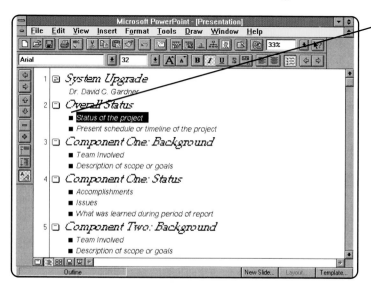

1. **Click** on the **first bullet** under slide 2. The entire line will be highlighted.

2. **Type New Service Contract**. It will replace the highlighted text.

Adding a Slide in Outline View

In this example, you will add a slide after slide 4.

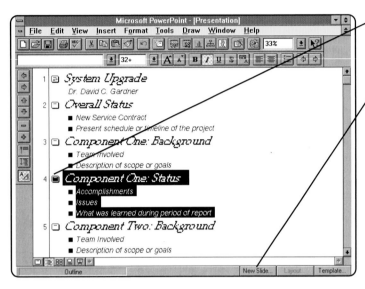

1. Click on the **symbol beside slide 4**. The text on slide 4 will be highlighted.

2. Click on the **New Slide button** at the bottom of your screen. A new slide symbol will be added and the following screens will be renumbered.

3. Type Component One: Network. Notice that it appears as a heading.

Adding a Subheading in Outline View

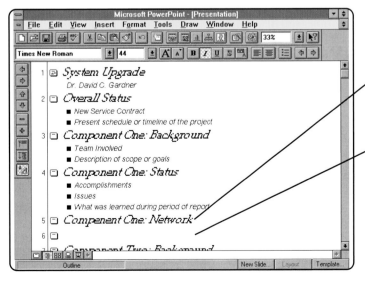

In this example, you will add a subheading to a new slide.

1. Click after **Network** if your cursor is not already there.

2. Press Enter. A new level will be added that is comparable to the previous level.

3. Press Tab. The new line will be converted to a subheading line.

SWITCHING TO SLIDE VIEW

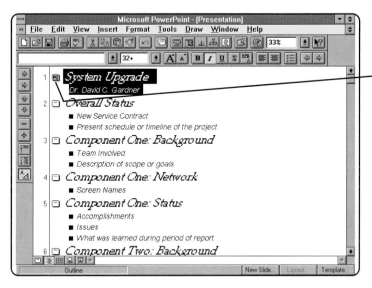

You can switch to Slide view at any time.

1. **Click twice** on the **symbol beside slide 1**. Slide 1 will appear in Slide view.

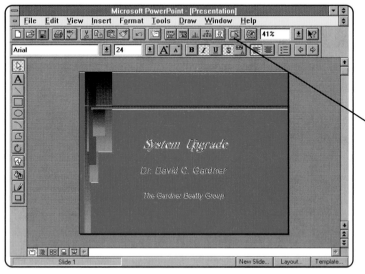

Notice that a predesigned template has already been applied. You can, of course, change this by using Pick a Look Wizard.

2. **Click** on the **Pick a Look Wizard button** in the toolbar. The Pick a Look dialog box will appear. Refer to Chapter 3, "Choosing a Predesigned Template," if you need help.

Customizing the Master Slide

You can customize a PowerPoint slide presentation very easily by editing the elements on the master slide. By adding or deleting text, changing the font formatting, importing a company logo, or changing the template, you can transform any of the Pick a Look Wizard templates into your own creation.

Customizing the master slide can be done at any time. But, changes you make on the master slide will affect all current and future slides in that presentation. Because the changes you make will probably have an impact on any design considerations, it's best to customize your master slide in the beginning. In this chapter you will:

❖ Create a new presentation using Current Format
❖ Change the font formatting
❖ Add text to a master slide
❖ Remove template elements
❖ Add a logo

CREATING A NEW PRESENTATION WITH THE CURRENT FORMAT

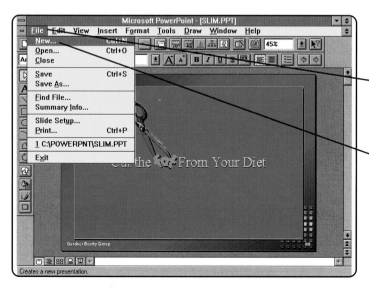

1. **Open slim.ppt** to slide 1 if it's not already open.

2. **Click** on **File** in the menu bar. A pull-down menu will appear.

3. **Click** on **New**. The New Presentation dialog box will appear.

4. Click on **Current Presentation Format** to place a dot in the circle.

5. Click on **OK**. A New Slide Dialog Box will appear.

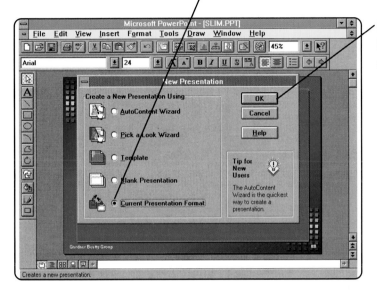

6. Click on the **Title slide** if it is not already highlighted.

7. Click on **OK**. A new slide will appear.

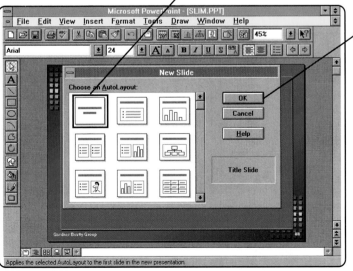

EDITING AND STYLING THE MASTER SLIDE

1. **Click** on **View** in the menu bar. A pull-down menu will appear.

2. **Click** on **Master.** A second menu will appear.

3. **Click** on **Slide Master**. The master slide will appear.

Changing the Title Font on the Master Slide

The text and text blocks you see on the master slide are called *placeholders*. They contain the font formatting information, but the words in the placeholders don't show as actual words on your slides.

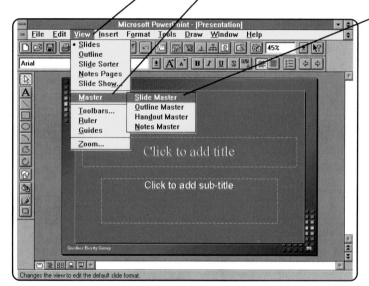

1. **Click anywhere** in the first line, **"Click to edit Master text styles,"** of the bottom placeholder block. An outline will appear to show that the text block is selected.

Notice that the font used in this line is Arial and the size is 32 points. The size will change as you continue to click on the "Second Level", "Third Level", etc.

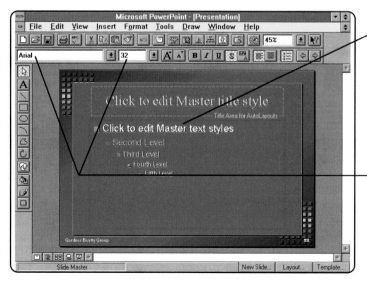

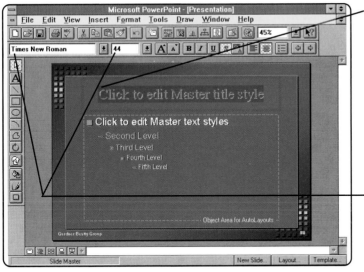

2. Click in the top text block to the **left** of the **C** in the "Click to edit Master title styles" line to place the cursor.

3. Drag the I-beam cursor to the **right** to highlight the text.

Notice that the font is Times New Roman and the size is 44 points.

4. Click on the ⬇ to the **right** of **Times New Roman**. A pull-down menu will appear.

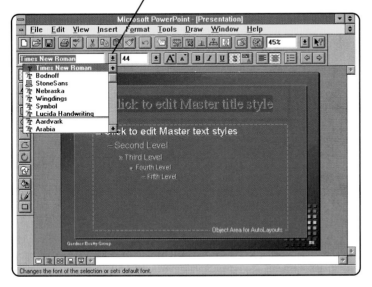

5. Click repeatedly on the ⬆ to scroll up.

In this example, **click** on **Arial**.

After the text is selected, you can change anything about the style of the text you want by clicking on the buttons in the menu bar. If you need help with these selections, see the section "Coloring Text and Adding a Shadow" in Chapter 6, "Working with Text Blocks."

ADDING TEXT TO A MASTER SLIDE

The placeholder text blocks that you see on the master slide hold only formatting information. Words that you type into a placeholder will show on the master slide, but won't appear on the presentation slides. You must create a new text block in order to add text to the master slide.

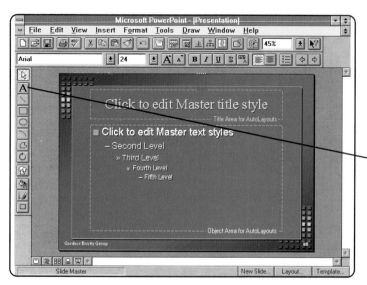

1. Click on the **Text tool** (the capital A).

2. Click on the **upper right frame** of the slide just above the "t" in "Master." A new text block will appear.

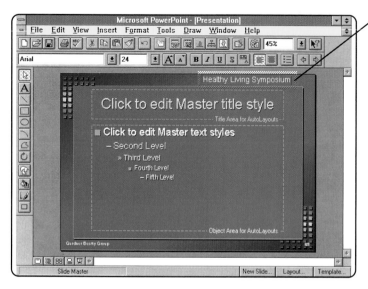

3. Type Healthy Living Symposium. Voilà! A permanent text block.

Deleting a Permanent Text Block

1. Click on the **border** of the text block. Handles will appear.

2. Press the **Delete key**. The block will disappear.

EDITING THE TEMPLATE

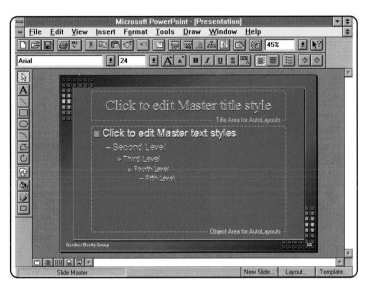

The templates you choose from Pick a Look Wizard can be customized on the master slide. It's simply a matter of selecting the elements, ungrouping if necessary, and then deleting and adding elements, to create your own version.

The elements that make up the backgrounds will differ on each template. In this example, you will customize the multboxs.ppt template.

Deleting Elements from a Template

1. **Move** the mouse arrow to the **upper left** group of **small boxes**.

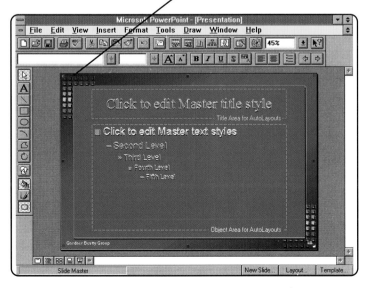

2. **Press and hold** on the **upper left** group of **small boxes**. You will see an outline of all the boxes in each corner.

3. **Release** the mouse button.

Notice that handles now appear around the border of the slide, showing that the element is selected.

4. Click on **Draw** in the menu bar.

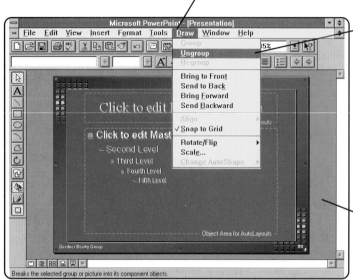

5. Click on **Ungroup**.

Notice that there are now two sets of handles. One is surrounding the center box. The other surrounds the corner boxes. This indicates that they are now separate elements.

6. Click on the **gray background** to deselect both elements.

7. Click on the **upper left group of boxes**. This will select the part of the design that contains only the small, colored boxes.

8. Click on the **Cut button** in the menu bar. All of the small boxes that were contained in that element, including the ones in the lower right corner, will disappear from the master slide.

ADDING A LOGO
TO THE MASTER SLIDE

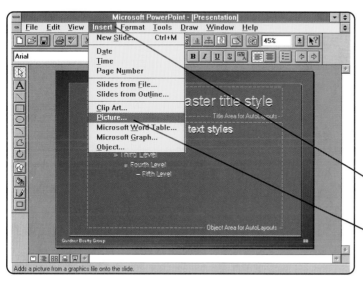

If you have a graphics file that contains your company logo, you can add it to the master slide so that it appears on every slide. The logo can be in .tif, .pcx, .bmp, or another format. The steps are the same.

1. Click on **Insert** in the menu bar.

2. Click on **Picture.** A Choose Picture dialog box will appear.

3. Click on the **directory** that contains your file. A list of all files in that directory will appear on the left.

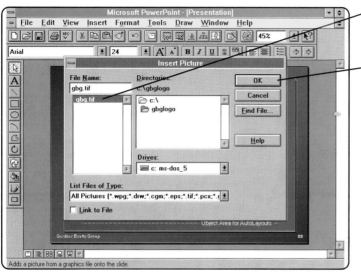

4. Click on the **file** you want to place.

5. Click on **OK**.

The image you selected will appear in the middle of your master slide, ready to be moved, resized, or grouped, as described in Chapter 11, "Working with Clip Art."

Program Manager

Part VI: Appendix

| Appendix: Installing PowerPoint 4.0 | Page 238 |

Installing PowerPoint 4.0 for Windows

This appendix will describe a complete, or custom, installation. In this appendix you will do the following:

❖ Install PowerPoint 4.0

Before you start, make sure that you have made and are using backup copies of your PowerPoint 4.0 Install disks. If you need help backing up your disks, see the *Power-Point 4.0 Reference Manual*.

INSTALLING POWERPOINT 4.0

1. Open Windows by **typing win** at the DOS prompt (C:>). The Program Manager opening screen will appear. Your screen may look different from this one.

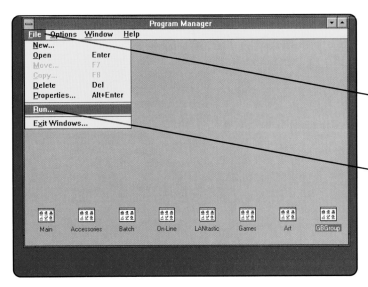

2. Insert your backup copy of PowerPoint 4.0 disk 1 Setup into drive A (or B).

3. **Click** on **File** in the menu bar. A pull-down menu will appear.

4. **Click** on **Run.** The Run dialog box will appear.

Notice that the cursor is flashing in the Command Line box. When you start typing, your text will be entered in the box.

5. **Type a:\setup** (or b:\setup).

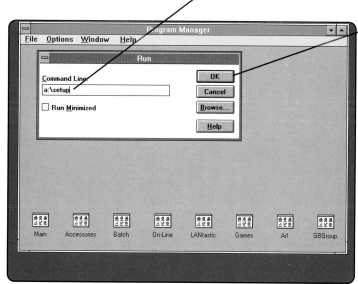

6. **Click** on **OK**. The hourglass will appear briefly with a PowerPoint message box that says, "Starting PowerPoint setup, please wait." Next, the Microsoft PowerPoint 4.0 Setup dialog box will appear.

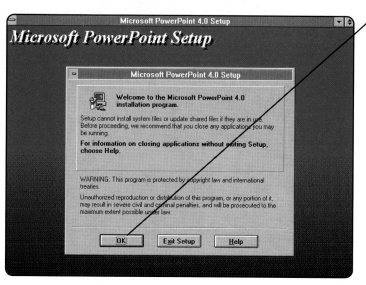

7. **Click** on **OK**. The Name and Organization Information dialog box will appear.

Notice that the cursor is flashing in the Name box. When you start typing, the cursor will disappear.

8. Type your **full name** in the Name box and then **press the Tab key** to move the cursor to the Organization text box.

9. Type the **name** of your **organization** if you have one.

10. Click on **OK**. The Confirm Name and Organization Information dialog box will appear. It will ask you to verify that the information you typed is correct.

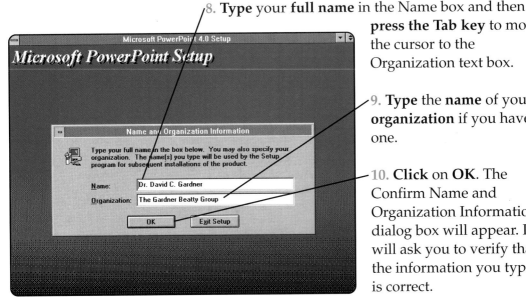

11. Click on **OK** if the information is correct. The Microsoft PowerPoint Setup dialog box will appear.

If the information is not correct, **click** on **Change**. The previous dialog box will appear. After making your corrections, return to step 10 above.

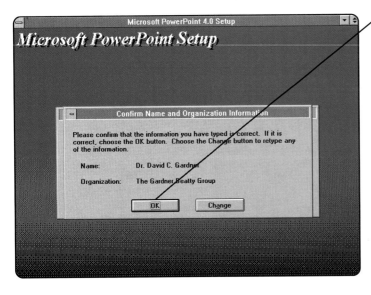

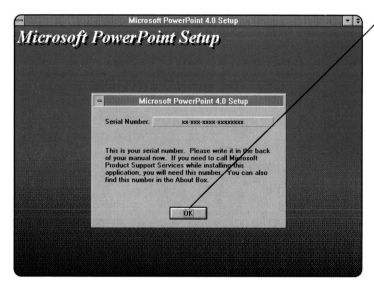

12. Click on **OK**. Your serial number has been electronically encoded on your disk for you.

The hourglass will appear again, along with the message "Setup is searching for installed components." Next a Microsoft PowerPoint 4.0 Setup dialog box will appear.

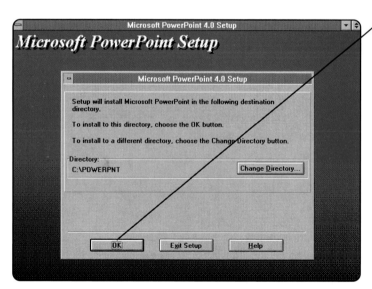

13. Click on **OK** if you want PowerPoint installed in the directory indicated.

If you want to change directories, click on Change Directory. The Change directory dialog box will appear. Click on ↓ to scroll down the list of available directories (and drives). Or type the name of the new directory in the text box. If the directory doesn't exist, a dialog box will ask if you want to create it. Click on OK. The hourglass and the "Setup is searching for installed components" message will appear.

14. Click on **Complete/ Custom** to follow the procedures in this book. This will automatically install all components of the program, including the Genigraphics driver. The Genigraphics driver is needed to send your PowerPoint files to Genigraphics, a service bureau that will produce the slides. Next, the Microsoft Complete/ Custom dialog box will appear.

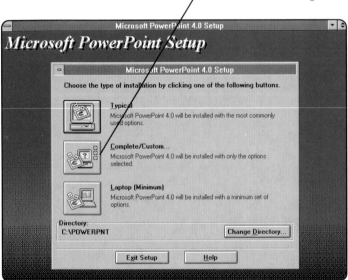

15. Click on **Continue** if you want all the PowerPoint options installed. The Microsoft Choose Program Group dialog box will appear.

If you do not want to install one or more of Power-Point's features, click on the option to remove the ✕ from the box.

If you remove an ✕ from a box, an additional Change Option dialog box will appear. It will allow you to select the specific features you want to delete (only some or all of the templates, for example).

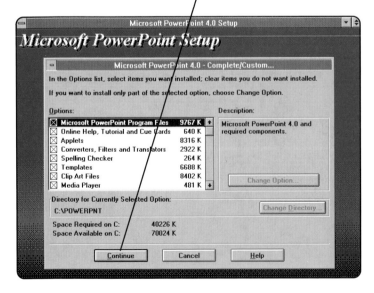

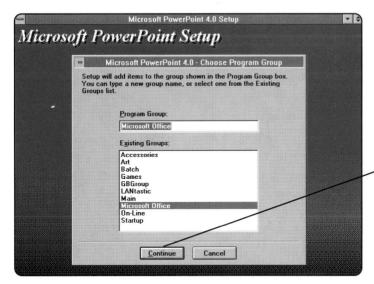

Notice that Microsoft Office is highlighted in the existing groups list box. If you want to put PowerPoint in another group, click on the appropriate group in the list.

16. **Click** on **Continue**. A Dictionary Options message box will appear.

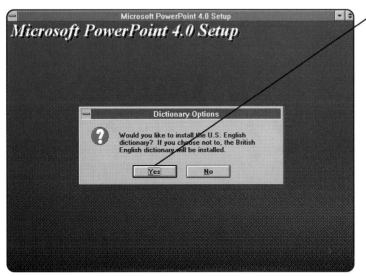

17. **Click** on **Yes** to add the dictionary. A message box will appear that says, "Setup is checking for necessary diskspace." Next, the Microsoft PowerPoint 4.0 Setup dialog box will appear.

At this point, you can sit back and watch the background information and pictures in the top half of your screen as PowerPoint copies files from the disks to your hard drive. The Microsoft PowerPoint - Disk 1 (2 or 3, etc.) dialog box will show you the percent of completion in copying.

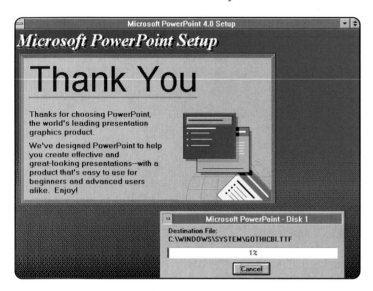

After PowerPoint has finished copying the files from disk 1, a Setup Message box will appear.

18. **Remove disk 1** from drive A (or B) and **insert disk 2**.

19. **Click** on **OK**. PowerPoint will begin copying the files on disk 2.

20. **Repeat steps 18 and 19** for disks 2 through 12.

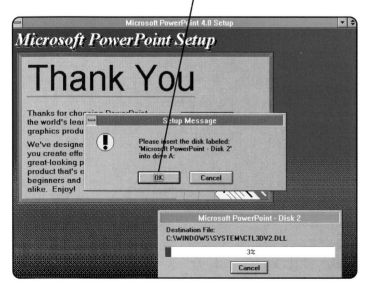

Note: Be sure to pay attention to the number on the diskette that PowerPoint tells you to insert. Toward the end of installing disk 12, you will see things happening as PowerPoint busies itself with the final stages of the installation. Don't worry! This means that you are almost done. Finally, the last Setup message dialog will appear, indicating a successful installation.

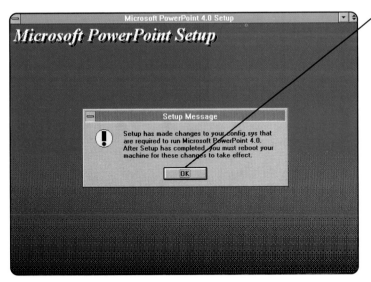

21. **Click** on **OK**. The Microsoft PowerPoint 4.0 - Restart Windows dialog box will appear. Click on Continue if you have no other applications open.

The Microsoft Office window will appear unless you chose to put Power-Point in a different group. In that case it may appear in a different size or location than the one shown below.

Congratulations! You have successfully installed PowerPoint.

ICONS, ICONS, ICONS, EGAD!

Wherever you chose to install PowerPoint, it will appear with all the icons you see here. Programs today come

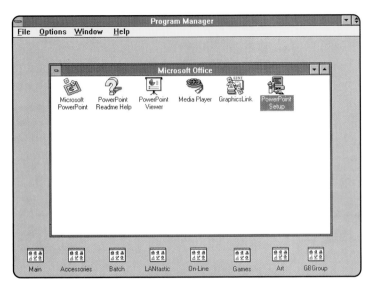

with so many icons that it's hard to keep track of the one that actually starts the program! A description of each icon is on the next page. we recommend that you move all the icons other than the Microsoft Power-Point icon to the Main group for safekeeping, just in case you ever need them. We never have, but who knows? If you prefer not to do so, skip this section, and go to Chapter 1!

A Quick Tour of the PowerPoint Icons

❶ Microsoft PowerPoint program icon opens PowerPoint 4.0.

❷ PowerPoint Readme Help contains information, since the printing of the documentation.

❸ PowerPoint Viewer is used to run slide shows. You can access this function through the menu bar. You will learn how to access this function on a computer that does not have PowerPoint in Chapter 17, "Taking Your Show On the Road."

❹ Media Player can run a movie or play sounds from a source such as a video disk. See your Windows 3.1 User's Guide for information on this program.

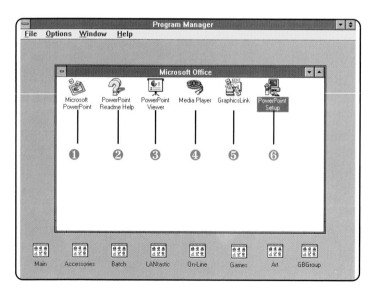

❺ Graphics Link is a telecommunications program you can use to send a presentation to Genigraphics by modem. This function is also available in the PowerPoint menu bar.

❻ PowerPoint Setup icon allows initial changes in the setup and maintenance of PowerPoint and is used when you uninstall the program.

Moving the PowerPoint Icon to Other Groups

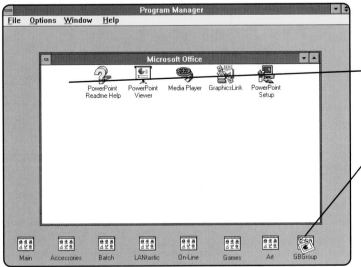

You can move icons from group to group at any time.

1. **Move** the **mouse arrow** to the **Microsoft PowerPoint icon**. (It used to be here, but we moved it.)

2. **Press and hold** the left mouse button as you **drag** the program icon to the appropriate **workgroup window** (ours is called the GBGroup).

3. **Release** the mouse button. The icon will disappear into the group icon.

4. **Repeat steps 1 through 3** to move the remaining icons to the Main group windows (or another holding group).

DELETING AN EMPTY GROUP

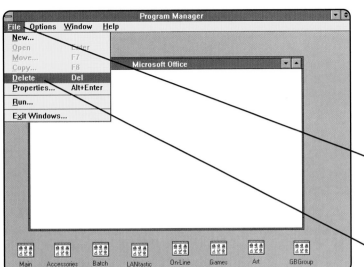

1. With the group open, **click** on **File** in the Program Manager menu bar. A pull-down menu will appear.

2. **Click** on **Delete**. A message box will appear.

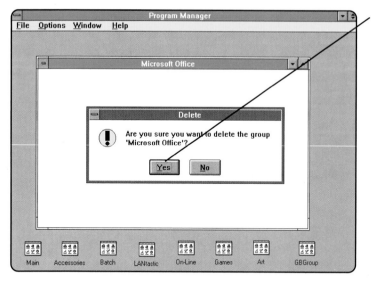

3. Click on **Yes**. The group will be deleted.

You're ready to enjoy PowerPoint. In addition to being a powerful program, it's a lot of fun!

Index